WHITE TIGER, GREEN DRAGON

WHITE TIGER, GREEN DRAGON

▼

A Tale of the Taoist Inner Alchemy

Simone Marnier

Authors Choice Press

San Jose New York Lincoln Shanghai

White Tiger, Green Dragon
A Tale of the Taoist Inner Alchemy

Authors Choice Press
an imprint of iUniverse.com, Inc.

For information address:
iUniverse.com, Inc.
5220 S 16th, Ste. 200
Lincoln, NE 68512
www.iuniverse.com

This novel is a work of fiction. Any resemblance of characters described therein with persons living or deceased is entirely coincidental.

ISBN: 0-595-12575-1

Printed in the United States of America

Epigraph

...the path of the green dragon and white tiger and the path of chastity run parallel. Those who engage in dual cultivation with deep sincerity are no less pure in heart than life-long celibates, for both have abandoned the trivial preoccupations of worldly men to seek an exalted goal.

The Abbot of the Cloud Valley Hermitage
(as quoted by John Blofeld in The Secret and the Sublime)

INTRODUCTION

To understand the cultural environment of *White Tiger, Green Dragon*, it is necessary to know at least a little about the Chinese spiritual tradition, Taoism. For millions, Taoism is a religion complete with gods, rituals and a priestly caste. But for many of these believers as well as millions of others in the six millennia since its inception, Taoism is much more. Whether one is religious or has no religious inclinations whatsoever, Taoism is a way of reconciling man with nature, understanding the Tao or Way which governs the cyclical patterns of life, and developing a spiritual perspective which, many believe, transcends the grave.

Like many other spiritual and religious traditions of the East, Taoism recognizes that the love of men and women is divine love in miniature. Throughout thousands of years of evolution, serious Taoist adepts developed the dual cultivation, a series of processes for using sexual energy to achieve greater spiritual depth and transcendent understanding. What in the West would have been condemned as either satanic possession or shocking licentiousness became in some Taoist monastic communities an accepted mode of spiritual refinement and religious practice. To most Westerners, it would be hard to imagine Catholic or Orthodox monks engaging in sexual activity with highly evolved women adepts in order to improve their own spiritual attainment. In fact, any one who would propose such a scenario through the centuries would probably be excommunicated, sent to an asylum or simply laughed at behind his back. And yet certain Taoist monastics not only saw no shame in sexual activity, but actually used the sexual act, from foreplay to climax and conception, as both a metaphor for and a vehicle to achieve complete mind-body awakening. Sex, like laughter, is an integral part of the cosmology of the Tao.

Taoists speak of their spiritual practice as "inner alchemy." Chinese scientists developed material alchemy, a forerunner of modern chemistry, with varying degrees of success. One type of Taoist practice involved using alchemical substances in an attempt to enhance spiritual understanding, not unlike the use of drugs in religious ceremonies by some Amerindian cultures, or the uses of psychedelics by spiritual adventurers in the 1960s. One could even suggest that the wine used in the Christian Mass may at some point have had a positive, alchemical influence on communicants in controlled situations. In Taoism, however, the symbolic language of alchemy took on a life of its own during periods in which the tradition was persecuted or subject to disfavor. Describing spiritual techniques in correspondence, scholars and monastics alike would use alchemical language as a code to describe the subtle process of spiritual transformation. In this lexicon, there was no physical "cauldron" or "firing process," and one did not physically compound a "golden pill" or create an "embryonic life." These terms represented exact elements of a Taoist yoga practice which, if followed, would lead to a kind of spiritual immortality beyond the narrow confines of the ego.

Sexual imagery also was used to describe the careful, controlled and often dangerous process of spiritual advancement. Among certain practitioners, sexual practices were employed, being far safer (and no doubt more pleasant) than eating cinnabar and deadly mercury (the cause of many an aristocratic Taoist's demise).

Of interest to students of sociology as well as religion was the role of women in the dual cultivation. Stereotypes lead us to believe that women have never held any lasting influence in Chinese culture, but in the spiritual advancement arts of Taoism, their power surpassed that of many priests, lamas and brahmans in other traditions. It was women alone who held the key to the inner alchemy and, with their inexhaustible reserves of spiritual and sexual power, unlocked the secrets of yoga for mortal men, often with humor and wit.

For thousands of years, the sexual yogas of China have flourished, despite the prudery of various governmental and religious authorities. *White Tiger, Green Dragon* was written to stimulate wider interest in this little known and often misunderstood subject. Readers expecting this small book to be soft-core pornography in disguise will be disappointed. Rather, it is a romantic, sometimes lighthearted, occasionally childlike fantasy about what might have been among the practitioners of the Taoist tantric arts a hundred or even a thousand years ago. Like the original White Tiger, Green Dragon practice it memorializes, this novel hopes to lead readers to something beyond itself, in this case to greater understanding of the many-faceted pathways to the Tao. Certainly, if nothing else, the dual cultivation warrants respectful recognition among those who value love and laughter, the arts and the natural world, and who are committed to ideals of justice, compassion, harmony and the highest knowledge, whatever it may be.

August 2000
The House of Three Lilies
Simone Marnier

CHAPTER I

▼

TU-MAI: THE GOVERNING VESSEL

He lowered the cup of tea from his lips with a silent smile while Shang Po, as she had for 23 years, tidied the table absent-mindedly.

"Stop fidgeting," he said, gently placing an old hand on her wrist. Shang Po looked up in surprise, for he had never reprimanded her before. Her drawn face softened into a smile, like his. It was no reprimand. "Drink," he said. She sighed.

"I have grown attached," she confessed lightly, as he patted her hand. "It is no matter," said Wu. He would miss her. But he was old at last, though it seemed it would never be. In the temple of the order he directed, it was important that he find younger partners to help him refine his energy and achieve wholeness.

"I will miss you," he said. She looked down at the worn, stone cups. Three leaves floated to the surface and swirled, autumn leaves in a pale green pond, presaging winter. He watched the lined face he knew so well, more intimately than his own. Together, they had played the sport of Mandarin ducks through youth, sickness, famine, now age. In the symbolic terminology of the Taoist canon, they had heated the inner furnace, mixing the elixirs of yin and yang, female and male essence, to create the spiritual embryo.

"Sometimes," she said, "I thought it was so much talk." He laughed, and nodded. "So it was," he replied, stroking her slender fingers. He would return to her in the village in spring and fall, he said, though his tantra with young girls now would now absorb him.

"I know a wonderful girl," she said, "though, of course, she has much to learn." Shang Po giggled. The Yellow Emperor was right, he mused: the essence of women is unlimited. She winked, "I will teach her. You will see."

He shook his head and wrapped both hands around hers. "I too have a student," he said, looking back toward the hermitage on White Crane Mountain. They looked at the mountain, mostly hidden in the lanquid blue-grey mist. "He is the finest student I have had," he said, his eyes brightening, "the best with books and alchemy, with a body like white jade."

Shang Po thought back two decades, to her first sight of Acolyte Wu. "Then he is ready, isn't he," she said, "to learn the Tao through the sexual yoga."

Their hands released, and Wu turned back to the table. Together, they shared one last cup of tea before departing, each to a separate destination.

*   *   *

For two days, Master Wu traveled the path to and up White Crane Mountain. Sometimes he rode the small donkey which was led by a village boy earning merit for kindness to old monks. Other times, he walked ahead, the cloth which was wrapped around his feet growing moist and heavy with spring dew. The climb was precipitous, but familiar. He enjoyed taking deep breaths of the damp, thin air, inhaling the sweet penetrating scent of new herbs, and trees in which the sap was beginning to rise. Each spring, each fall, the ritual was established, and welcomed. His energy level, like many of his order, was remarkably high, and there were many times he had to tap the boy playfully with his walking stick to keep him moving up the barely discernible path.

On the third day, taking a sudden turn to avoid a tangle of roots, they practically fell against the door of the monastery. After some time (too long, thought Wu), the gate opened.

A startled monk bowed nervously. "I am sorry, sir, I did not know…"

"I would return so soon? There's reason for your concern?"

Wu gave the boy a penny and a blessing, and watched with delight as he scrambled away.

"If only we could keep that store of ch'i lifelong," he sighed, "we would not have to trouble ourselves so!"

The young monk relaxed a bit and smiled, bowing until forced to stop by Wu's walking stick. "Please come in, venerable sir. There is tea and dry clothing." Wu nodded. It was not time for a lesson, nor to assess the mischief invariably rampant during his absences. Today, he would rest and hear reports from his assistant. Tomorrow, he would focus on the education of Tu Ming.

*   *   *

The first rays of dawn fell across the painting of Ancestor Lu in Wu's private meditation chamber. The first birdsongs brushed his ear, blending with the inner harmony which absorbed his mind. His eyes gradually regained their focus and he noticed that one of the fat white candles had gone out. Stirring, he missed the warmth of Shang Po's cozy house where he had spent so many months in what seemed an interminable expanse of years. His feet were cold, and he had gotten out of the habit of warming himself through concentration. Very well, he would do so now, while it was spring, an easy time to renew the practice.

Wu rang the bell beside the unlit candle and, lifting the folds of his robe from his sinewy calves and ankles, stood steadily, gulping air, biting his teeth to revive the circulation in the manner taught to him by his master.

One of the boys sent to the monastery from poor families arrived with pale green tea, rice and pickled vegetables. Such an earnest face! Wu could not repress a smile. He placed his strong, wrinkled hand on the boy's head. The boy looked up with vacuous black eyes, bowed clumsily and darted from the room, as if afraid he could not contain his manners and good behavior for more than a few seconds.

Wu's eyes followed him through the doorway and out of doors, across the courtyard, gradually taking in the larger view of the monastery as it awakened in the mild spring air. Things were in somewhat greater disarray than when he had left. Sweeping left undone, little piles of dirt and debris swept but not yet disposed of, bedding from guestrooms left hanging from the window. Who knew the extent of neglect of duties and personal development among the monks and novices? Perhaps the promptness of the morning rice was a ruse to attract attention from other inadequacies! If so, Wu's aptitude for shrewd assessment had been sorely underestimated.

But while noting the lack of discipline, even in the deportment of the monk who greeted him and the boy who brought him his tea, Wu did not make a judgment. Taoist monks were not like Confucians or Buddhists, who (in Wu's mind) put too much stock in form and not enough in substance. Under the lackadaisical eye of his surrogate, the supply of wine and rice paper surely would now be low. The grounds, as far as he could see, suggested abandon and overgrowth, not the precision husbandry he had once observed on the grounds of a Ch'an temple.

Wu turned back into his chamber and sat at the table, where he closed his eyes and sipped the hot tea. Another smile came to his lips. The cold, clear water of the White Crane Mountain springs made an unequaled brew. If only he could bring this freshness back to the hermitage, reenergize it and reawaken the community's zeal for experiencing and living in the Tao. In some ways, it was easier to cultivate a spirit of eagerness and commitment during a period of war and strife. The current era of peace and tolerance encouraged laziness and sloth. Soon it would take fresh blood to awaken the hermitage out of its gradually growing somnolence.

Eyes still sharp for his years, Wu saw Ming at the far end of the hermitage, speaking to one of the other monks. Ming looked up in the direction of Wu's chamber, then back to the other in a few moments' conversation before bowing and walking resolvedly in wu's direction.

Even now, Wu mused, he outshines the sun. He is the one I have pegged all my hopes on, he thought. Soon I will retire from this community and return to the village to live out my final years with Shang Po (though she does not know it) and cultivate my essence to assure an advanced age and high attainment. Today, as Ming knows full well, is the beginning of his initiation, the prerequisite to mastery and leadership in our order: the White Tiger, Green Dragon. Wu's eyes closed briefly in a paroxysm of pain. For while there exists no higher path to divine knowledge and ecstasy, similarly there is no path more fraught with danger and potential for annihilation than the tantric yogas. In a sense, Wu would have felt more at ease leading his most prized student to vie with martial arts masters and skilled archers than the yogas that flow through the treacherous currents of human sexuality.

*   *   *

Ming stood silhouetted in the doorway and bowed low. The two men did not exchange words, but a strong charge of love, mutual admiration and devotion passed between them. Wu looked fondly on his favorite student. The younger man was taller than most of the other monks and possessed of a clear, untroubled countenance. Still, there was an undercurrent of dark passion in his eyes which concerned Wu greatly. That passion, expressed on numerous occasions during scholarly debate or practical differences over ethical issues, led time and again to Wu's greatest fear: that this very intensity, combined with unprecedented temptation, might wrest Ming away from him and dash his hopes in the world of dust.

Ming had all the potential requisites to succeed Wu as presiding master except for this unpredictable store of unspent passion. Unleashed, it could, Ming feared, undermine not only Ming's own cultivation—so perfectly evolved at present—but also take down with it the entire hermitage, which, like so many other Taoist monasteries, lay precariously poised between fulfilling practice and destructive eccentricity.

But perhaps his was a melodramatic assessment. It was just this passion, after all, that produced the heat to warm the cauldron in which Ming could produce the spiritual embryo, described in Taoist literature. Certainly, Ming had studied the internal alchemy in theory for the past eight years. Now, in the Year of the Dragon, it was time to put theory to practice. Reaching his hand into the fire, he will be burnt. But as surely as passion serves knowledge, he will heal and, drawing from his years of training and experience in the other yogas, will perfectly master the internal arts.

Wu looked critically at Ming as he entered the chamber. He was graceful, strong and well formed, but not one of the hermitage's celebrated athletes. His greatest virtue was in the clarity and brightness of his unwavering mind. His powers of concentration, his compassion for all living beings, his voracious love of learning all impressed those who knew and worked with him day by day. While he could run, wrestle and climb as well as any other monk in a tradition which prized physical wholeness, it was this combination of intellectual openness, a loving heart capable of great feeling, and a wry sense of humor which made his presence treasured by all who knew him.

Ming had come to the hermitage as an adolescent and remained in training, and in teaching the younger monks, for nearly 10 years. His father, a civil servant, was in exile, and his mother had been honored to give up the brightest of six children to the security and good care of the hermitage. To Wu's knowledge (and it seemed conclusive in this matter), Ming had never slept with a woman. It would have been better if he had. Wu scowled slightly. Perhaps he had been wrong to shelter and protect this sapling so tenderly. So relentlessly. There were so many variables.

"Master. What is troubling you?"

Wu waved his hand to abort the annoying round of ritual bowing. "Sit down," he said. Ming sat across the table from his master on the lower stool. He watched with curiosity as the furrow left his master's brow and the frown half-melted into a wistful smile. It was a message he could not fathom.

"Was it a difficult journey? Is there news in town?"

Wu closed his eyes and shook his head. When he reopened them, they were bright and merry. "Here," he said. "Please have some of this poor monk's tea."

Ming bowed again and accepted the bowl. It was a great honor to have tea in the master's chamber.

"Tu Ming, I fear I have too long deferred your initiation into the dual cultivation. Let us not delay. I am writing a letter of introduction this morning to Madame Chang of The Yellow Bud."

Ming gulped hard. "The Yellow Bud? But master, that is…rather, I have heard that it is…"

"A brothel. Yes, yes, and a highly regarded one in Hsienyang." The hermitage had had an arrangement with the brothel dating back before Wu's arrival at White Crane Mountain as an adolescent in the early years of the Ch'ing Dynasty. Madame Chang would see that Wu's spiritual heir was introduced to the sexual arts in a supportive, nonthreatening environment. Ming was not a shy man; in fact, Wu had seen him bathing and noted the novice's delight in his own lean, well muscled body. It was a body designed in Heaven for the dual cultivation, Wu had speculated, not like his own bony, awkward form, gangling and nervous when he first entered The Yellow Bud so many years before.

Wu had lost many novices over the years at this stage—most of these decided to leave the order and take wives, but they always returned to the hermitage on feast days and pilgrimages and with only a few exceptions came back for several months every so often as married monks, to practice what level of the internal alchemy they could master. For in this tradition, it was considered unnatural for a monk not to be familiar with women. What some Buddhists and others called "chastity," the Taoist tradition of the White Crane Mountain Hermitage considered a pathological condition; in a sense, it meant estrangement from the essence of the Tao. And on those who practiced the White Tiger, Green Dragon, it conferred a kind of immortality.

Other novices had bloomed under The Yellow Bud's care and, once comfortable with their own sexuality, had successfully formed partnerships with women of the village willing to earn spiritual merit (and a much needed stipend) by coupling with monks several months out of the year. Since the tantric method involved no ejaculation, few of these partnerships resulted in the birth of children—only five or six in the 20-odd years Wu had supervised such matters—so there was little erosion of the hermitage's financial resources.

Wu had little doubt that Ming would progress well under The Yellow Bud's tutelage, though there was always the possibility that his voluptuous nature could boil over, spoiling the cauldron for good. It was best, however, not to dwell on what could be. Already he must be thinking about finding a suitable partner for Ming when his apprenticeship with Madame Chang was completed. Someone experienced with monks, someone devoted to the Tao, but plain, even homely and not particularly young. Possibly a woman known to Shang Po, or that hermitage staple, the matron Su Ba. Wu had not kept up on the list of girls and women who (for the most part) sought out this honor and yielded up their infinite store of merit for the development of monks in search of enlightenment. As Ming grew older, he would need the vitality of young girls and virgins to increase his spiritual power; for now, a doughty housewife familiar with every nuance of tantric art would be of greater value.

Wu lifted his cup to his lips, and Ming followed suit.

For many conflicting reasons, it was for Ming a moment of great anticipation and no little anxiety.

*   *   *

"Master, what can I expect in Hsienyang?"

"Have you not studied meditation for 10 years as advised by Liu I-ming and alchemical theory for eight?"

"I have."

"And have you had visions?"

"Visions of great horses, black and white, like the t'ai ch'i, locked in mortal combat. Visions of exotic flowers, such as those the goddess tends in her garden on the moon. Fragrances, like patchouli and balsam fir, only more intoxicating, maddening in their intensity."

"And lights?"

"Meteor showers more astonishing than those chronicled by science. Explosions of stars, sunbursts, lightning that rises in clouds, like the spores of smashed puffballs. An aurora of many colored crystals, twisting, clinking, sparkling in the cold black depth of infinite night."

"And what did you do about these visions, Ming?"

"I let them wash over my consciousness, as the sea rakes the shore. I paid them no heed, and have experienced the pure bright clarity of my inherent mind."

Wu nodded. It was not a pat response, but an honest and unconventional answer from an original mind. All the masters, from Chuang Tzu to the Ch'an teacher Hongren and the Indian yogi Patanjali had given the same admonition. In meditation, let the visions play themselves out and vanish, and focus instead on the changeless essence of mind.

Wu looked long at the pale, handsome youth before him, so perfectly arrived already at what to many traditions would be the ultimate destination. And yet in this order, he thought, you must go further into yourself in order to more perfectly become one with the great source of being.

"You have achieved all that can be realized here. Tomorrow morning, you and the servant Yun will retrace my steps from yesterday, down the White Crane Mountain to the village and just beyond, where the Wei River flows. I have consulted the oracle; there is no more auspicious day or hour for your journey."

"The planets are in my favor," said Ming. "Is there anything that I should do in preparation?"

"Everything that you will need has been identified and will be ready for you at dawn. You know the theory of our tradition well. But I do not suggest you interview others in our order regarding their experiences in the art. Though, of course," he added with a mirthful turn to his lip, "you may already have done so. No, today, you would be best served by immersing yourself in contemplation of your essential nature. Meditate, my son! And do not forget: whatever may befall in this period of initiation, you must strive to 'keep the mouth of the dragon dry.'" Wu curtly dismissed him with a brush of his hand. Ming arose, bowed and left the chamber quickly. A breeze stirred across the courtyard, ruffling his orange robe and disturbing the thick black hair in his top knot. He was gone in a few seconds, a sleek gazelle. Wu looked down into his tea bowl, but there were no leaves to read. He sighed, and rang the bell to summon the serving boy. Then, to no one in particular, he erupted in a roar of solitary laughter that almost scared the serving boy away.

CHAPTER II

▼

HUI YIN: THE PUBIC REGION

Uncharacteristically, Tu Ming's mind swam in and out of speculation as he sat in the full lotus before the temple altar. Though the day was bright, the hall was dark, punctuated by several squat candles with disproportionately hearty flames. The murals of past Immortals gleamed on either side, not with the radiance of shelac but rather from the encrustation of centuries of grime. "And so our perceptions make filth itself beautiful," Wu had once told him. But it was a dangerous philosophy sometimes, something Ming would not have dared to utter within these walls. Filth can be perceived as beauty, evil as good, poison as nourishment, and death itself a doorway to life. Ming was not so sure. Despite the ubiquitous image of the t'ai ch'i, the two black and white teardrops locked in the circle of an eternal, pseudosexual embrace, perfect balance and harmony did not seem an ideal to attain if it meant, in the sage's words, that happiness must be rooted in misery, that the underpinnings of comedy are tragedy. How could one aspire to personal perfection, or more important, to help others in the journey through life, with the cynical philosophy that honesty inevitably turns to dishonesty, that goodness succumbs to vice. Even when the tide turned and these proclivities reversed themselves, falling back on the irresistible gravitation of yin and yang, how was it possible to evolve, or even to live as an ordinary man, knowing that the seeds of degeneration were planted even in the noblest act?

Ming let go of the thought, as he had told Wu he did in meditation, and entered the state of pure, objectless awareness. This, after all, was the key, leaving the realm of opposites entirely and communing directly with the universal mind. But what kind of answer was this, his own "little mind" (as Wu called it) interjected, if it required one to live in monastic discipline for 10 years only to be told that the journey to self awareness had just begun? How natural was it if such unnatural discipline, carried out in the unnatural protection of the hermitage, were required to experience a level of reality which should be available, as a birthright, to all?

Ming's eyes opened, stemming the inward light that flooded his heart, and refocusing on the murals of the Eight Immortals caught in their eternal dance beneath the patina of smoke and wax. Not a monastery incubated pedagogue among them! Wu and Master Shan both had chided him for thinking too much. But why be equipped with the subtle, celebrated power of reason and not employ it? And wasn't it Wu who (so he had heard) so often extolled Ming's intellectual attainments to his teachers and even to visiting masters? If there was balance here, Ming failed to see it. Instead, he saw a confusion which must be resolved if he were to succeed Wu (as he suspected he one day would) as master of the hermitage and teacher of a new generation of monastics.

At least today there was a new focus for his inquiring and restless mind. He wondered why it had taken so long to progress to the state in which he was ready to begin the dual cultivation. Perhaps it was just this restlessness, this accursed ability to see the obverse of every premise and to persistently question dogma (even in this least dogmatic of traditions) which caused Wu to push the date ever ahead. Was he even now prepared? His friend Li Feng, a less advanced student in every score, had long since gone down to the world of dust to engage in the tantric arts. Or was it, as Wu suggested, simply a matter of the stars? Once again, Ming let the thought go. It was not productive to endlessly speculate. Invariably, Ming's reasoning to the contrary, Wu was correct in whatever course he recommended. How did he always know? He was like Lao Tzu's sage prince, ruling his kingdom as subtly as one would saute a small, fine-boned fish.

The time of unproductive deliberation was past. Ming knew that his real work lay ahead of him. More than Wu realized, Ming knew something of the delights of the body and their potential to deceive, distract and destroy. On the other hand (here the active mind rekindled), this was in fact the life force most completely in tune with the Tao, the essence without attributes which gives life to all things. Within the tyranny of the t'ai ch'i, the dark yin gives birth to the bright yang. Ming knew the hazards awaiting him at the establishment with the innocent sounding name, Yellow Bud (though he knew, as a Taoist, that this was a code name for the real generative force). While Madame Chang and her charges undoubtedly were good women, with the best interests of the hermitage in mind, this would be the most difficult stage in his study of the tantric arts. Every variety of sexual delight would be presented to him, and he would have nothing but theory and a lifetime of spiritual and physical discipline to sustain him.

The process would be all the more treacherous since he was required to abandon himself to sexual knowledge, willingly sacrificing the essence he had so assiduously cultivated as he pursued both the limits and limitlessness of his virility. It was at this time, he knew, that many novices were lost. His stay would be a short one, less than one month's time, perhaps only a week or two, but potentially enough to undo a lifetime of discipline, to break possibly forever his link with the reservoir of universal mind he could tap into at will. His apprenticeship called for him to work in the village as a copiest to conserve his physical powers by day, and by night, to deplete, if necessary, his store of energy to gain the knowledge required to build it up again. So like a person taking a dangerous and potent drug, he thought, that he can develop an immunity to its power in the future. Only much more than that. Because it was not immunity he was looking for. It was absolute union with the eternal, without change, without fluctuation, in this life and for all time.

Ming breathed deeply and rhymically, as a visiting master from the West had taught him, and remained immobile in clear minded meditation until dusk. Then he rose from aching limbs and went to gather his satchel and a few hours sleep before the servant Yun came to fetch him at dawn for the trip on horseback down the mountain to the river town.

                    *   *   *

The ride down White Crane Mountain was uneventful and smooth, except for a few periods of rain showers, and, for Ming, the unaccustomed discomfort of spending one night in a rocky grotto. Yun watched Ming with mischievous eyes as they shared a meal of rice with pickled vegetables and tempeh beside one of the clear streams that made the wonderful tea Wu loved. Ming shot him a questioning glance.

"Excuse me, venerable," said Yun, clasping his carton of cold tea with relish, "but I cannot help but envy you your upcoming adventure. Many merchants would pay handsomely for just this opportunity."

Ming smiled ruefully. After more than a thousand years, the dual cultivation still was misunderstood by the people. And with good reason. To the masses of people who struggled to make ends meet, the lofty philosophy of the internal arts surely sounded like nonsense. "Internal alchemy." "Creating the spiritual embryo." "Mixing the golden pill." What did that mean to men who lived lives of virtual slavedom, trying to wrest a crop of vegetable mallows from a small patch of rocky land and tending to the never-ending needs of a wife and 10 or more children? It was fate that had singled out Ming for the rare opportunity to enjoy a fine education at the hermitage, to explore a wisdom tradition extending back to the Yellow Emperor and to develop an interior universe unknown to the great preponderance of humanity. But nothing in the culture of certain Taoist monastics evoked more gossip, misunderstanding and ribald humor than the dual cultivation. While it was generally acknowledged as a kind of sacrament which enabled monks to achieve greater spiritual attainment, the specifics were so cloaked in mystery and secrecy that inevitably misunderstandings and apocryphal legends rose up around the subject . For nothing so fascinates the human mind as to speculate on the covert sexual activities of other people. For many, therefore, the dual cultivation was a euphemism for license and debauchery, all within the sanitary context of ecclesiasticism. Some clicked their tongues in disapproval, but most who held this opinion snickered wickedly behind their sleeves.

"An adventure, yes," admitted Ming, sizing up a companion which most monks would not have bothered to talk to. "But what do you know of the tantric arts?"

Yun wiped a shabby cloth across his grizzled chin. "You hear a lot, you know? But who is to say what is true and what is not? Now, you. You know, I suppose? I mean, they teach you, what? How not to 'lose your chicken?'" Yun guffawed and threw back his head at the thought of sanctimonious monks studying the avoidance of premature ejaculation.

Ming grinned. "Not exactly, my friend. You know something about our routine, our way of life. Would you say that it is particularly licentious or lewd?"

Yun was taken aback. "Ah, no, certainly not, venerable. A good lot, all of you. A bit slack at times," he winked, and Ming nodded, knowing he referred to the sometimes careless cleaning, husbandry and grooming habits of the community, especially in Wu's absence. "And I have to say, I haven't seen no boys and girls smuggled into the grounds for illicit purposes, like you hear in stories. No women around neither. With all respect, sir," he bowed in case he had spoken out of turn, "all I know is that I keep busy enough, escorting your kind up and down the hill, running errands for the old one. But still…there must be something in it. Is there anything you can tell me…just to cure my ignorance, of course!"

Ming had no sensational tales to tell, but, because in his innocence he believed all people were essentially good and entitled to know truth, decided not to let the conversation conveniently dissolve into silence. "As you must surely be aware, my knowledge is theoretical only."

"Oh, theory's just fine, venerable, considering you're going to have some of that practice any day now!" He squinted with merriment and shook his shoulders at some unspoken, lascivious imagining.

"Well, it's really very simple," said Ming, struggling to find ordinary words for something which was really quite extraordinary. "Just as a man and woman can unite to create a physical child, so the combination of their essence can lead to the formation of a spiritual embryo. By meditating and practicing certain techniques, this embryo will grow within and lead the practitioner to a higher level of being." It sounded pretty stupid when stated bluntly. The tradition was so full of subtlety that it resisted translation into easy platitudes. He decided to stop while he was ahead and follow Yun's cue.

Yun wrinkled his nose and tilted his shaggy, unwashed head. He scooted closer to Ming, who recoiled only slightly at the odor of Yun's old clothes and scruffy body. "It that it? Isn't there any more?" Yun scratched his head and tried to focus on thoughts which had no context for forming. "Isn't there any sex to it?"

It was Ming's turn to laugh. "Quite a bit, I'm afraid. But that falls into the practical part. You know, Yun, we men don't have the answers to what you and I both would like to ask. Perhaps you should direct your questions to someone who really knows the subject: a woman!" he added mischievously.

Yun's eyes popped in horror. "I'm asking no woman nothing of the kind!" he said.

"Well, where did you get your undoubtedly superior education in matters of the bedroom arts? From a school master? Your father? Your friends (though I am sure they had much to say on the subject!) A monk?"

Yun was not about to answer. Obviously, Ming had hit a sensitive nerve. "No, Yun, if my knowledge is correct, you learned it from a wife, a mistress, a pillow girl. So it will be with me, as it has been with generations of White Crane monks. We leave for a time our superior male bastion of learning, spirituality and culture, and descend into the world of dust to sit at the feet of mere women who can teach us the arts that transform ecstatic pleasure into immortality."

"Hmmph," snorted Yun, "I'd be content with just some of that pleasure! Well, I don't see as to what your kind can learn from women. It's men who teach them a thing or two! But forgive me, venerable, I forget my place when we talk. I appreciate your kindness, but still don't understand a word you've said!"

Ming nodded a smile. "Well, I should meditate a while. Stand watch will you?" The waxing moon behind a stand of pine trees interspersed with mountain laurel. Crickets began to chirp; the horses grew still. Yun went off a pace to relieve himself, while Tu Ming turned his face to the falling sun and half-closed his eyes. Why was it so difficult to talk about the tradition, and so delicious to practice it? If only all men could as easily and wondrously fall directly into the experience of universal mind, without having to know so much before hand! Would it be the same for him when he mastered the White Tiger, Green Dragon? Or would his fall—as he feared—be deeper, and into an inextricable vortex pulling him away from, instead of into, the light?

*   *   *

Madame Chang tapped her fan impatiently on her writing desk. The payments from the monastery had been late. It was becoming a pattern, this slatternly disregard for meeting one's obligations. It was different when Master Wu had a firmer grip on things, before he began spending so much time away cultivating his essence. She sniffed contemptuously. What was in it for The Yellow Bud, really? The girls did not turn into immortal fox spirits. If anything, their quality of their lives was reduced by this tiresome activity. Some may have thought their store of merit increased as they coupled for hours on end with self-centered monks. But most had the good sense to see it as only another series of acts to perform for the customer. Well, the pay had been good, and who knows, the spirit world undoubtedly did smile on those who helped the realized ones achieve a higher unity with the Tao. Still, a woman could not go through life just being a crucible in which some sexual deviant pounded out the golden pill! Madame Chang was a shrewd businesswoman and knew it full well. If I were a man, she had thought throughout her 20-some years in the profession, I would have a series of successful inns, flower boats and brothels to my credit. Now, I struggle to keep the local merchants well provided with sensual pleasure and have to deal with a half dozen other-worldly Taoist monasteries which only pay after a good pilgrimage season. Thanks to the gods that there still a few good patrons like Liu Geng and his sons and nephews to allow The Yellow Bud to retain the accoutrements for which it was renowned.

Well, let them be that way, she thought, biting her full lower lip and pushing an unsatisfactory billing scroll back into its niche. No longer would she release her best girls to work with monks just starting the dual cultiva-tion. She clapped her hands for the serving girl. "I need to see Mei Cha," she told her curtly. The servant scurried from the room, recognizing a potential tempest in her mistress' eyes. Mei Cha had been in training with one of the older women since joining The Yellow Bud the previous spring. She was a quick study, there was no doubt as to that, but lacked the advanced skills which fetched a higher price from the more experienced practitioners. There were silk merchants in town this week; she could not afford to waste pre-cious time and talents on incontinent monks who occupied the house for days, and paid with empty words and blessings weak as pauper's tea. And Mei Cha lacked the necessary artifice to pretend she enjoyed a patron's attentions. More than once, a client had joked that despite her command of her art, she never really seemed to have a good time. Hah! As though any of her employees ever had, except when exchanging stolen kisses with the other girls. No, pretending to enjoy the sexual act, as well as the beatings (usually gentle, but sometimes out of hand), humiliations and (perhaps worst of all!) having to listen to boring stories about the clients' manly exploits, was one of the most important parts of their work, leading to higher fees, happier customers and better assignments. The other girls called Mei Cha "Little Willow," because even her smile was sad.

"Mei Cha," she said, when the child arrived, "come here. I have a challenging assignment for you." She looked coolly at the girl, impeccably gowned in yellow silk. The bruise over her right eye had almost healed. Her hair was clean and glossy, though plainer hairpins would have to do.

Mei Cha bowed. "I am honored, madame, with whatever service I can perform."

"Has Sei Kuan instructed you completely in the White Tiger, Green Dragon?" Madame Chang pressed her lips together firmly and waited for a reaction. As usual, Mei Cha revealed nothing. At least she has command of her feelings, Madame Chang mused wryly.

"Yes, I know it well. I have been privileged to join her with monks from the Jadestone Temple. I know the theory…you may ask Sei Kuan, who will recommend me. All the stages and techniques to use with the five personalities and the seven levels of attainment are familiar to me."

"And have you practiced this yoga yourself, with monks?"

"I have. And I believe it has been successful for them."

"Though of course you would have no way of knowing!"

"They would not say so, certainly. But I believe it is something you feel, you can tell. I could sense when his practice was assisted by my participation."

Madame Chang nodded. This was good, she would do. "Then it is settled. I have a new monk for you, someone who, I am told, is a virgin in every sense of the word, though rather old to be in such a deplorable state for a man, I'd think. I am tired of wasting my best girls' efforts on these pale-faced monks, so here: I am giving you a treat. Something in which you can divert and prove yourself for a week or two, or perhaps longer. Just think of it: no more drunken dockworkers, or plowmen with hard fists, or spoiled sons of minor officials. At least not for the period of this relationship. What do you think of that?"

For a moment, a glimmer of emotion did play on Mei Cha's porcelain features. She was tired of the hard life she had been thrust into by reason of her parents' poverty. This, if done well, could result in better opportunities in the future. She appreciated the motivation of the monks, even if they were clumsy and uncommunicative. Certainly, it was better than the drunken lust she more often encountered, though it had to be admitted that the inebriated advances of louts lasted only a short time, while the plodding monastic alchemy often seemed interminable. Perhaps she could learn something of this peculiar philosophy herself. There was no doubt that she needed something larger than the squalor of her day to day existence to sustain and give meaning to her life.

"Yes," she said, "I would gladly do it. I know exactly what needs to be done with such a man."

"Good," said Madame Chang, satisifed for once with this beautiful but previously disappointing protegee. "Then it's settled. He will be here tomorrow. He will visit me as usual and then meet you for his initiation. This should work well for both of us. I'll save a significant amount of money, and you may find yourself with a stream of customers more in line with your temperament. Go get some rest…you will be needing it!"

Mei Cha bowed and turned.

"And Mei Cha," Madame Chang said.

The girl looked over her shoulder.

"Try to pretend you're enjoying it. OK?"

"Yes, madam, I shall." And Mei Cha almost smiled.

*   *   *

Tu Ming said nothing during the second day of the journey down White Crane Mountain. Having learned nothing titillating from the previous day's conversation, Yun was content to ride alone a good pace ahead, ostensibly to watch for bandits and wild animals, none of which appeared. A faithful servant of the hermitage, despite his coarse appearance (which Wu had said made him think of an itinerant Taoist mendicant he had known), Yun kept a close enough eye on the monk and listened for breaks in the rear horse's footfall. He knew that look of dignified impassivity, having seen it often enough among the monks he served (or shepherded, as he liked to think of it). Deep thoughts, he mused, not of this world. Not something I am likely to experience in this lifetime!

For Ming, however, the serene dignity of his countenance masked an internal state of anxiety mixed with elation. Throughout his life, a nameless desire had haunted him. Surely, it was not something as simple as the need for sexual companionship, though, to be sure, the two impulses were related in some seminal way. Wu had looked into his heart, and seen the inferno that raged within. "To all appearances, you are as serene as the Old Boy," Wu had once said, referring to Lao Tzu, "but your eyes give you away! I wish I could rid you of this hunger or offer some words which would fall like waves of cool water on the flame that eats away at your heart." The hunger did not die; instead, it grew, rapacious. The fire, which at once cheered and awed him, was contained so long as he practiced meditation and gave himself up to the universal mind. But even then, the ache persisted: "There is more, there is more," it whispered. "Beyond even all this, there is more."

The travelers passed through the village where Shang Po was sweeping the floor of her cottage after the evening rice and continued to Hsienyang, always visible by its twinkling lights to Wu when he left her bed before dawn. Now it was dusk, and Ming's horse, drawn by memories of water and hay, had taken the lead, knowing the way to the hostel where generations of Taoist monks had stayed during the most critical stage in their internal development. Ming took a deep breath of the clean, riverside air, filled with the wonderful smells of fish, damp cedar and sweet flag. "It is as though my entire life has been preparing me for this moment," he thought, then, catching himself, closed the latch of the speculative "little mind" that made even the most profound concepts seem noisy, trite and confusing.

Entering the hostel, the two men were greeted by the innkeeper Shieh, a dark giant with broad, exaggerated features. He was busy bickering with several of his suppliers when he noticed Ming. "Ah, another monk!" he shouted, though it could have been his everyday voice. His face contorted into a look of both cunning and lechery. "I've been waiting for you." He walked around Tu Ming, looking him up and down. "A bit late, aren't you?" he asked with deliberate double entendre.

Ming smiled softly and bowed. "Please excuse the delay, innkeeper. For me, it has been an unfamiliar journey, one, perhaps, not unknown to you?"

Shieh thought a moment, then guffawed and slapped Ming powerfully on the back, surprised that the slim form was unshaken by the assault. "That's good, that's good. I like you....."

"Tu Ming. I have traveled two days with this man, Yun, as I am certain you have been told."

"Yes, yes, it was just all this fuss with these thieves I call my suppliers that caused me to forget. Yes, yes, well, you're right, there is a journey which you are making for the first time and for which I...well, I could be the tour director!" Shieh and his business colleagues (who were now catching on) roared at the innkeeper's incomparable wit. Ming bowed again, wrote his name quietly in the register and found his room, the uproar at his expense vastly entertaining the men he had left behind. Like the Tao, some things are best when "not spoken," he mused, slipping into his quarters for the night and for an unspecified time to come.

*   *   *

The dragon and tiger are none other than yin and yang, the female and male. They are the cauldron and furnace of alchemical literature, the medicinal substances required to compound the golden pill. The cauldron, cool and limitless as the element Water, fills herself and nourishes the Fire that would not die. You have read in the Great One of the miraculous pass, the portal into all knowledge. I will tell you what this pass is. It is none other than the inexhaustible female. Must I be blunt? Can you grasp the concept of the dragon and tiger, water and fire, cauldron and furnace, pestle and mortar? The mysterious female is the key to the firing process. This talk of base metals into gold and drinking an elixir of mercury is not the real alchemy. Enter into her and take it into yourself, again and again. Lao Tzu said, "The valley spirit is the mysterious female. Her door is the root of heaven and earth." It replenishes itself continuously. There is no coercion, but it is freely given. Opening up, you will enter the cinnabar chamber where all knowledge is stored. Conserving your essence, you will draw her into yourself, up through the lower and middle tan tien into the seat of ecstasy. Here you will find madness and death…or the knowledge that will give you eternal life.

*   *   *

A light cool film of perspiration coated Tu Ming's jade white body. He sat in the meditation posture facing the east. Gradually, the golden light washed over his skin, giving him the other worldly sheen of a temple deity. All thoughts of why and wherefore, questions which delighted his sharp intellect during regular consciousness, evaporated; his mind was clear and luminous, his individual ego was subsumed in the infinite, his insight into the nature of things enlarged as he experienced a transforming sense of oneness with the Tao. Instead of fatigue from his journey, Ming found himself preternaturally alert in a high state of awareness and arousal.

By mid-morning, Ming had gone to the scribe not far from the hostel to let him know he would be available for copying and calligraphy in a few days time. Next, he found The Yellow Bud but a half hour's walk from the scribe's quarters, discreetly tucked between the edge of the city and a stand of willow trees where the river sloped and turned, branching into rivulets. Like many houses of its genre, it had a poorly maintained exterior, possibly a deliberate neglect, so as to not call undue notice to the house, but, once the door was opened, a kind of bourgeois splendor surrounded the visitors. Ming bowed to the servant who invited him in, as well as to an altar with red candles, prayer notes and incense sticks, and sat for a refreshment of tea and salty noodles.

Madame Chang watched him from behind a curtain. Her first impression was one of surprise, for he was older and more poised than any other monk sent to her for the initial training. He has known women before, she mused, a half-smile on her lips. He is too beautiful. Perhaps it is with other men that he has practiced the bedroom arts. Mei Cha will tell me. But he glows with more than worldly charm. This monk is different, she thought, and spent longer than she intended watching him drink his tea and take in the unfamiliar surroundings.

"Venerable sir, I am Madame Chang," she said abruptly, parting the curtain. "Welcome to my poor home. I am unworthy," she said, according to the prescribed formula, bowing low, "to entertain and instruct so illustrious a scholar and adept!"

"The honor is all mine," returned Ming, rising from the chair and returning bow for bow. "It is I who am unworthy to pass this threshold to accept your hospitality."

The two stood tall and looked clearly into each other's eyes. There was an honest exchange of information and mutual respect for which convention had no words or gestures. Madame Chang turned and took a basket from the servant.

"Please, venerable sir, take this basket and return at dusk with it filled with cherry petals. Do you know the park?" Ming nodded. "There you will find what you need. When you return, you will meet your partner, Mei Cha. She is looking forward to assisting you in your cultivation."

They bowed again, and Ming left, walking through the city to the gardens which lay beyond.

He spent several hours exploring Hsienyang with its bustling businesses, rickshaws, the cries of children (an indecipherable Babel of merriment and pain) in a high-pitched banter with female relatives. He noted the scent of noodles cooked in fragrant fat, the apothecary shops crammed with jars of spices, mushrooms and dead lizards; and everywhere, the dank humidity of the river, which clung to one's clothes, one's very breath. For a time, he sat on a wharf far from the workmen, lest they take offense at what would seem like an elite monk disdainful of the rigors of physical life. But the life of a monk was rigorous, too, requiring strenuous training to wrestle, not with carp, but with the Tao itself. How many men could endure such a life? And was he comparable to the challenge, now that he was away from the security of the hermitage and about to pursue a new level in his education? Ming let go of the doubt, the insecurities. Come what may, he had never felt more in tune with his own being. And, though he did not know it, he wore his preparedness like a talisman, for several men and women stopped and bowed as he passed by, and vowed to make the pilgrimage to some holy place they had long deferred, such was the charismatic beauty of his bearing.

When he reached the park, Ming pulled a scroll, brush and ink from his sleeve. "Fallen from now bare trees, cherry petals, soft as silk, powder the earth," he wrote. "Earth, once naked, is clothed; heaven, once clad, is exposed. When will I return to the nature I had before delusion clouded my pure mind?"

*   *   *

Evening fell. Crickets began to saw their songs. Madame Chang smiled at Ming as they sat in her parlor, a pot of pale green tea between them. She heard the arrival of the brothel's other guests ("the paying kind," she thought warmly). Her mind fluttered from thought to thought; his mind focused entirely on the present moment. She talked politely about The

Yellow Bud and her long association with it, but Ming could see beyond her eyes, into a heart that was not very deep and filled with intrigue and a level of curiosity whose object he could not fathom.

"And so you are part of a noble tradition of monks and seekers who have availed themselves of our special services. I take it you are familiar with tantric technique, at least in theory?"

Ming did not answer immediately, searching her heavily painted face for some trace of understanding. "Like others before me, I have studied the internal alchemy for many years."

"But you must admit, venerable sir, that the dual cultivation requires a special, shall we say, affinity?"

"Once one knows the firing process, what difference does it make if the cultivation is of heaven or of earth?" He saw he had offended her. "Please, there is no offense intended. I have on every authority heard of the superior partners you provide, especially at the introductory stages of this particular cultivation."

Madame Chang was annoyed. "Perhaps, then, you are not such a beginner after all, given your age?"

Ming bowed. "I am honored to have accumulated additional years of training and what I hope is wisdom before embarking on this precious journey," he said. "May each of us approach the eternal mystery at all times with beginner's mind."

Madame Chang clapped for her servant and summoned Mei Cha. "Then this should work out well," she said cooly, rebuffed in her search for more information about this enigmatic guest. "Beginners should learn together. I trust you will earn much merit during your visit here, or, failing that...." she smiled with the satisfaction of having the last word, "not too sharp a detour from your destination. Good evening, sir."

Ming sat in silence for some time until he heard a slight swish behind him. He turned and looked up at Mei Cha, her head lowered, a veil over her face. She was very small, enveloped in a robe of bright blue silk. Mei

Cha held out her hand which Ming took, feeling a kind of electric shock throughout his body at the touch of her soft, cool skin.

"Please come," said Mei Cha, the gossamer veil fluttering over her lips, sculpted to every breath. "Please let me carry your basket. You must be tired. We shall go to the bath."

Ming bowed and handed her the basket with his other hand. How easy it was to let go of the tyrant mind, he thought, but so hard to let go of a young girl's hand.

Mei Cha led Tu Ming to the bath, her head kept low, the sound of her silks murmuring like water. It was still early; the moon was nearly full, framed by a moon-round window overlooking the pool. The other guests would not come this way until much later. They had the dark room, punctuated by lanterns and washed in the final golden glow of twilight, entirely to themselves.

"Please let me bring you a robe and towel," she said, pulling away gently. But Tu Ming did not let go.

"Tell me who you are," he whispered, drawing her near, "tell me what you know, why you have taken this path, how you—a prostitute..." She cringed slightly at the word. "...can indoctrinate monastics who have spent a score of years in scholarship and meditation...."

"Please," she said in a pleading tone, "please stop." She let the basket drop. Its petals spilled at their feet. Her finger went to his lips. "Haven't you heard of the teaching which cannot be spoken? Must you spoil the ritual with talking? The ritual is all we have!"

He put his hands on both sides of her head and slowly slid the veil upward, against and over her chin, her red, painted lips, her cheeks, the eyes, the moth-like eyebrows and over her head. The veil fell to the tiles below, among the petals.

"If I am to know the truth by this practice, I must know the agent of its revelation," he said, holding her head up toward his own. She looked into his eyes, unafraid. He was not a client like the hundred others she had served in such a short period of time. He was more like a peer, someone like herself. She had never regarded a male in that way before. Every man had made her feel even smaller than her small stature. If she had had a brother, would he have been like this?

Ming looked long at Mei Cha's upturned face, finding there the signs of understanding so utterly lacking in Madame Chang. "Please forgive me," he said at last, releasing his hold, sliding his hands down her arms and lightly grasping each small hand. "You are right. I am here to learn from you. But can't you see? It is important to know by what authority our masters teach us. You are only a woman, a young girl. What can you possibly know? And since my masters tell me that I will learn the most important practice here, then surely you must know! But how? What is the source?"

"What is the source of anything," asked Mei Cha, "of life, of feelings, of the lot fate gives us? I am no sage, venerable sir, but a poor girl, a prostitute as you have said. I have been trained, that is all. There is nothing more."

"There is more," said Ming, "but perhaps, as you have said, it will be revealed outside of the domain of words. Forgive me." He bowed again.

Mei Cha nodded and released his hands. She walked to the cabinet at one side of the pool and drew out a green silk robe, a towel and brush, and took them to the monk.

"Please allow me to take these old things," she said. He bowed and turned his back to her, facing the water. With sensitive, expert fingers she undid his top knot, removed his cap and loosened the thick black hair around his shoulders. She unclasped his robe and tunic, and eased them down his arms, around his waist and let them drop to the floor, averting her eyes in the event Madame Chang were to suddenly appear demanding strict accordance with protocol. Ming looked down and stepped out of his garments as the luxurious swathe of green silk billowed over him and wrapped him like an embrace. He breathed slowly and deeply, grateful for the practice which gave him steadiness and poise in situations where, on their own, body and mind would crumble.

Tu Ming turned to Mei Cha, who took his hands and sank with him onto the cold tile at the edge of the pool. She gathered the strewn petals and pushed them into the water. Tu Ming scooped up a handful and lifted them to this face, inhaling their subtle bouquet. When she saw him do this, Mei Cha smiled. When a man or woman with a solemn expression smiles, the impact can be disarming. Tu Ming was touched and lifted the petals to her, as an offering, then halfway through the motion, impulsively cast them into the pool. Mei Cha laughed.

"Come," she said, drawing the towel and brush to a dry place along the rim. She moved to the edge and sat where the moonlight fell through the round window. Unloosening her robe, she slid soundlessly into the warm, mild water. Ming dropped the robe so recently acquired, and slid into the water beside her. Their heads and shoulders bobbed in the moonlight.

"Do not say it…whatever it is!" Mei Cha said, with almost a giggle. "I feel you may have been here before!"

"I will say it," he whispered into her ear. "I have been here, but not in this place. Do you understand? Have you not been 'here' before as well?"

Mei Cha looked with sudden longing at his broad white shoulders and up into the black, insightful eyes. She marveled at his reserve, his quiet power. Where was he, even now? But words were not her tool, and she must not forget why she was here. She carefully wrapped her arms around him and placed her cheek and body warmly against his as the water clucked and splashed beside them.

*   *   **

It was to Ming's detriment as a student of the tantric arts that he had difficulty using Cha as a tool of his development. Though she was only a woman, he saw a parallel in their lives. Cha was sent to a brothel at a young age because her family could not afford to keep her. Ming was sent to a monastery at about the same age for the same reason. Of course, it did earn more merit for a family to send a boy to become a monk than a girl to become a prostitute, but what choice did they have. There were few convents, and celebate nuns were generally regarded as a disastrous waste of precious life essence. The brothel was the only possible choice for a girl of Cha's dim prospects. Ming shuddered to think he might have been born a woman. But then, if he had, being only a woman, surely he wouldn't have thought much about it, or about anything for that matter. Ming thought about Cha's life as he copied documents in Wei Fan's small shop. What a curse it was to be born a woman, only to think about painting one's lips and cheeks, and deciding what robe to wear and how to serve tea. Or worse yet, to marry a cruel serf, bear children in great agony, see many of them die, till fields, cook coarse food, grow ugly and die young without having known the first thing about the Tao...a sorrier state Ming could not imagine. In comparison, a prostitute's life was probably a blessing.

But any way he thought about it, he could not think neutrally about Cha or the tiring, artificial coupling to which he was being subjected. He smiled to himself as he swept his brush to make a particularly graceful character. Well, it would probably take some serious cultivation to undo the damage of several of their briefer encounters in the past two weeks! He had been taught that the second day of the full moon is the only day of month men can have normal sexual relations without damaging their ching (essence), but had not learned how difficult it would be to resume detached cultivation on the third day and thereafter. Nonetheless, Ming felt that in the loss of control, rather than the endless plodding prescribed by tantric theory, he was closer to the Tao, no matter what Wu had told him. "You must concentrate, concentrate at all times!" the master had warned him. "If you lose your concentration, it is mere coupling, and your finite store of essence will be depleted." When he was younger, such admonitions filled him with apprehension and the resolve to exercise detachment and restraint at all costs. But now, he was not so sure. Cha was a person, someone he liked from the start. She was not just an inexhaustible reservoir of immortal cinnabar, good for nothing but to yield up her essence so he could compound the golden pill. She seemed genuinely interested in his life, what he believed, what he was trying to achieve. He let his thoughts drift back to the previous night's cultivation.

$$* \qquad * \qquad *$$

"When have you been sleeping?" she asked him. It was halfway between midnight and dawn, when he would leave.

"It is no problem. I have trained to sleep a few hours here, a few hours there," Ming said, pulling the covering over their shoulders. He noticed again a strong scent of jasmine in the loose tresses of her thick hair. "Our schedule is quite regular. We sleep in the early night, arise at midnight, practice, sleep, rise at dawn, and so on."

Cha regarded him with interest and, for the first time, a little pity. "I am sorry. That is such a horrid life."

"Horrid? You call the practice which leads to the highest knowledge horrid? And what of your own existence, is that what you prefer?" He was amused to note how her caution had abated and her impertinent spirit had begun to express itself more boldly since their first meeting.

"Prefer," she said, with disdain. "I have no choice as to what I prefer. This is a distasteful life, it is true, but it is better than starving or living with a man who would beat me every night. You have talked to me about freedom, how you cherish it above all else. Yet you live a virtual prisoner. Not even your sex life, which all men cherish, is free!"

Ming sat up, offended. It was Cha's role to teach him the rudiments of the dual cultivation, yes. But nothing else. What else could she possibly teach him? Why was he disturbed by her questions?

"You say that only followers of the Tao can be free, but I see nothing but bondage, perhaps worse than the bondage of the serf to his plot of land," she persisted. A frown surfaced on her forehead; Madame Chang would not approve. "At least the serf has the flexibility to flow with the changes of the seasons and the pace of his own body. You, you are at the mercy of intolerable 'masters' who create artificial hardships in the name of discipline!"

"That is not so!" protested Ming, then, reflecting, "well, perhaps. Perhaps it is so...but only in part. But be careful that you do not criticize what you do not know. How can you know what I have gained or not gained from this regimen of discipline? Have you ever meditated on the sublime Tao?" His tone was earnest and intense, but he did not berate her harshly. "Have you undertaken a schedule of work, contemplation and rest designed over thousands of years to lead to the supreme goal? It is true that you have been taught—and probably rather quickly!—the tantric arts, but do you know the meaning behind the technique? What does it mean, to fuse cinnabar and mercury and to create the union of heaven and earth?"

"I cannot match you wit for wit, my venerable sir," she admitted, "but neither am I blinded by indoctrination! To give up the self in the act, as I have done, as you have done on three occasions, perhaps that opens our hearts more to truth than the mechanical repetition of strokes and the unnatural breathing practice I have taught you. Perhaps I am responsible not for your advancement, but for your decline!" Cha was somewhat perturbed, and placed her hand gently on his arm. "Of all the men I have served here, you are one I would least want to offend in any way."

Ming was touched by her solicitude and, though he did not know it at the time, the seed of restlessness already planted in his nature would be encouraged by her naive but affecting words.

"It has been said that breathing is more important than eating and drinking," said Ming. "When we tune the energies of our being with the rhythm of our breath, we are in a position to achieve great insight. Mei Cha, do not forget to be mindful of your breath, not only during the cultivation, but at all times. Find moments to spend in meditation when you leave the unhappiness of your life behind and enter into a transcendent state of awareness."

"I know what you mean," she said, with a small smile. "My hours with you, they are my meditation. Though I am puzzled by your life—you could be a civil servant and an illustrious public official! (Ming laughed)—you are a presence of peace and understanding such as I have never known. I will cherish these times we have together and reflecting on them will be my meditation when you are gone. But as I will, as you have taught, be mindful of my breaths, so please be mindful too that you do not become a parrot! You will not find the Tao, I am certain, by copying the formulas of your 'masters.' Now, come," she said, placing his hand on her naked waist, "let us work on your golden pill until the first rays of dawn. Then I can sleep and recoup my energy and you...."

"...and I shall have your energy to sustain me for another day!" he said warmly, rolling softly into a favorable position.

*   *   *

Lust must be entirely avoided and renounced during the practice of this art. The act replicates the union of heaven and earth, and the birth of the 10,000 things in the womb of the formless Tao. Coarse essence (sexual fluid from both partners) must be conserved and transmuted into subtle essence by causing it to interact with energy and spirit. The cauldron is the lower cinnabar field (below the navel). The male in union must raise his nourished essence to the upper cinnabar field so as to flood the brain with transformative light. Through this light, is the deathless knowledge attained in this very lifetime.

*   *   *

For several hours by day, Ming copied documents in Ts'ao Sung's small, cluttered office. Unlike the innkeeper Shieh, Sung did not exactly leer at Ming at intervals throughout the day, but would smile nervously and turn away, as though to prevent himself from breaking into an embarrassed laugh, whenever he brought the monk a new assignment. On several occasions he commented on Ming's pallor, asked if he was getting enough rest and, as though fearing he had overstepped propriety, put his hand quickly to his mouth and hurried to the other corner of the room. Ming took a deep breath, looked for sympathy to the statue of Kuan Yin in the office shrine and continued to dip his pen in the black pool forming on the inkstone.

"Venerable sir," Sung said one day after several weeks had passed, "I have this message from your monastery." He handed Ming the small scroll. Ming put down his brush, wiped the ink from his fingertips and accepted the message with a short bow. Sung smiled nervously and skittered off. It was a message from Master Wu:

"Acolyte Ming, I have received reports through various sources that your initiation is completed and that, if you stay longer, you may be in peril of the ultimate distraction. There is nothing more for you to learn at The Yellow Bud. I expect you to leave the morning after you receive this message. You have reached a critical stage in your training where only the support of the hermitage can sustain and develop you. I look forward to seeing you before the next full moon."

Ming read the message twice, put down the scroll and sat quietly for several minutes, letting thoughts of the most extraordinary three weeks of his life flood his mind at random. Suddenly, he was aware that Sung was watching him, though pretending to pore over a court document.

"Mr. Ts'ao, pardon me, but today must be the last day I enjoy your hospitality and the opportunity to practice my small art in your employ," he said bowing. Sung nodded, secretly surprised and a little saddened that his young assistant, who was so meticulous with his assignments, soon would be gone. "Your excellent work will be missed, venerable sir," Sung bowed in return. "Come, put your work aside, and have some tea."

Ming too was surprised the message had come so soon. The past few weeks were like a reverie, a dream. Had he progressed much further in his quest for unitive knowledge of the Tao? He wondered. Certainly, he had learned the techniques, under the guidance of a congenial if not especially enlightened apprentice-teacher, which would sustain his practice for many years to come. Suddenly, it swept over him, a tide of enormous misery: years of wandering from partner to partner, engaged in the difficult and possibly thankless couplings which would produce no child, no pleasure, only the unexpected muscular fatigue in his groin and back, and the constant vigilance to preserve and persevere. Perhaps his teacher in the tantric arts was right: he trusted the words of his masters, the tradition of his order more than his own common sense. Ming sighed, and sank back against the hard chair. He missed Mei Cha, though he should not have. At this stage, he was expected to have had times of loss of control. And those times were indescribably wonderful, though they threatened to topple everything he had worked so hard to develop in his years at the White Crane. But his training and personal commitment to knowing were a more powerful force. He knew that future partners would not only be sterner critics of his performance, but would provide information to Master Wu which could be damning. Ming drank his tea in silence, and thought ahead to the last night with Mei Cha which lay ahead.

*   *   *

Mei Cha arose late and sat at her table to paint her eyebrows into the sweeping, moth-like arches which men loved. What was this "unity of all things" Ming talked about? It must be real enough to the men (and women, she had heard) who gave up every human delight, even sexual pleasure, in its pursuit. What she had learned through hearsay over the years, as well as the lessons she had received in the mechanics of the dual cultivation, seemed to accord with Ming's descriptions of the path which led between the valley of opposites to the sublime knowledge beyond appearances. Still, it was terribly abstract. She sighed. Shouldn't the natural be what is clearest and easiest to understand?

A servant came to her room with a message from Madame Chang, who wanted to see her immediately. Cha put the finishing touches on her lips, slipped into her robe and hastened to the madame's chamber.

Madame Chang was bristling, obviously annoyed by something, when Cha arrived, bowing apologetically for any delay in responding to her summons. The madame's face wore an expression of veiled contempt as she turned to greet one of the lesser of her employees.

"The monk, Ming," she said curtly, waiting for a reaction.

"Yes, madame, he is doing well, an excellent…"

"He is not doing well. He is leaving. And that means I will be getting a smaller fee."

She paced across the room. "Am I to believe that you have had something to do with this?"

Mei Cha's mouth opened in protest, but Madame Chang waved her hand for silence.

"As you might know, I have my ways of knowing what goes on between my sheets," Madame Chang said. "It would seem to me that without this monk's constant attention to the lesson at hand, you would have abandoned your charge altogether and relaxed into idle reverie! Isn't this so?"

Mei Cha took one of the deep breaths she had practiced with Ming, learned partly from her theory, partly from his experience. "No," she said calmly, looking from the floor up to Chang's cold eyes, "I taught as my lessons were needed. But I learned as well."

Madame Chang laughed. "It is not your station to learn, girl."

"I must learn as I teach or I am no teacher," said Mei Cha, growing in confidence. "I was placed in the role of a teacher of the tantric arts with only theoretical knowledge and general sexual experience to guide me. The monk has been helpful in assisting me to assist him…and, it is my hope, future monks who come here to learn the White Tiger, Green Dragon."

Madame Chang's lips pressed together tightly. The girl was being difficult, but what she said made sense. When did she learn to use her head? Did this monk have something to do with it?

"You and this monk…you have talked too much. Monks do not come here to learn from your words, but from your body."

"My body and my words express the same truth," said Mei Cha. "I cannot pretend to take this cultivation seriously unless all parts of my being are engaged. This monk Ming has informed me that this is true, in the scriptures of his tradition."

"I would not worry about scriptures, if I were you. You will never learn to read. You are here to bring men to heaven in one way or another."

"Excuse me, madame, but he will be here shortly."

"Yes, and that shouldn't be any concern of yours!" said Madame Chang swirling about and facing her dramatically.

"What do you mean?"

"I mean," said Madame Chang with a taut smile, "that I have asked Li-Shang to warm your monk's furnace tonight. You may take whatever of these merchants the others do not want." Mei Cha could barely conceal her great disappointment.

"But madame, surely this will have a disastrous effect on his energy, vitality and spirit! His master will notice the change immediately and complain, perhaps not even pay!"

"I think the change will do him good," hissed Chang. "You have become arrogant and impudent in the past few weeks. That will not do. If you would continue to master the precious tantric arts which I and your betters have taught you, you had better remember your place! Do you remember Lieh Wan? It was not by her choice that she became the girl I sent men to who wanted a little rough play! You are very young, so I am charitable. Despite your youth and inexperience, I will keep you on in this specialty, but only if you humble yourself to me and to our guests. What do you say to that?"

Mei Cha knew she was beaten. She took another deep breath and bowed her head. "I am honored to be in your employ, madame. I have no choice but to follow your direction."

"Good. Then go to Li-Shang and make the necessary arrangements. I trust your patron this evening will have no need for your learned conversation!"

Mei Cha left, her face flushed with an anger which she was not permitted to express. She hurried to her room and was about to ruin her makeup in a fit of tears, when she managed to get a grip on herself and think about the situation. Li-Shang was a reasonable woman, well practiced in the tantric arts, but also vain and fond of expensive things. Mei Cha opened the secret drawer under her makeup tray and produced one of several small opals given to her by an elderly government official during her early weeks at the brothel. "You are a tender child, with few defenses," he had told her amiably. "Use these as you need help avoiding difficulties in the future." She had to spend this last night with Tu Ming, not only for his sake, but also for her own. Though there would be hell to pay if Madame Chang learned of the deed, she would pay Li-Shang the sum of one opal to exchange partners that night.

*   *   *

Ming looked sadly at Mei Cha as he took her small hands in his. She had secured a private room not far from the bath where they began their work together.

"You have taught me a great deal, little flower," he said, raising her fingers to his lips. "What will happen to you now that I am leaving? Will you continue to teach others?"

Mei Cha withdrew her hands and undid his topknot with a placid smile. Smiling charmingly in difficult situations was an art acquired during her training as a pillow girl. "Yes, thanks to your tutelage, I now understand more fully the wheel of opposites, how good arises out of evil, how evil arises out of good, and the path which leads to the great peace within our hearts. The questions I have asked, you have answered, by throwing them back to me and encouraging me to use my own resources to understand."

"But it is still a bit of a mystery, isn't it?"

"Yes," she admitted candidly, "I cannot pretend to fathom everything you have told me." The air was cooler this evening; she wrapped the silk cloth around both their bodies.

"Your mind is as fine as your body," he said, "your spirit is still unsoiled. Is there no other way for you than to remain here?"

Mei Cha closed her eyes and breathed deeply. As he can control the depletion of his essence, so I can stop my tears and smile, she thought to herself. "If my mistress permits, I will continue to work on this cultivation with others of your tradition. I, too, will grow."

"I wish…no," he said, catching himself. Mei Cha's role was an important one. She could not be linked to any particular devotee. As for himself, he knew he must continue his work with women with greater mastery of this practice. Master Wu was right: this was the most treacherous stage. Only in recognizing perfectly the long-term role of each partner could the dual cultivation be continued to its ultimate end.

"What do you wish?" she asked, looking for the last time deep into his dark eyes.

"I wish you to fully partake of our practice tonight. Let go of the theory, forget the numbers, the hours. Enter into my breath. Take my energy as I take your essence into myself."

When dawn's golden glow fell upon the pool, they were exhausted, near sleep in each other's arms. Mei Cha was grateful that Madame Chang had not discovered her ruse. "I am grateful, too," she whispered to Tu Ming, "that you have opened my mind."

"And I thank you," he responded, "for opening to me, for the first time, the Gate of the Mysterious Pass."

CHAPTER III

▼

CH'UNG —MAI: VESSEL OF THE UNINHIBITOR

Summer was a busy time for the White Crane Mountain Hermitage, as it was one of the sites of the Stork Cloud Festival which drew hundreds of pilgrims each year. During this time, several shamans and magicians from the province arrived at the monastery to prepare for their part of the festival, which added color and excitement to the otherwise quiet, peaceful environment of the White Crane community. Wu enjoyed the activity, the smell of spicy new dishes cooked in his kitchen by visiting chefs, the tinkle of bells and the tuning of ch'in strings in preparation for the lively weeks ahead. The extra administrative work was passed along to his assistants, Lao and Kai-t'i, allowing him the freedom to wander among the tradesmen and the showy magicians so loved by the people. Each year, the festival drew more pilgrims to White Crane, assuring that there would be rice, quilts and fuel to get the monks through another snowy winter, with some left over to supplement the monastery's small but excellent library.

The festival, rooted in ancient regional folk traditions, attracted a wide array of pilgrims and sightseers, most of whom followed a pastiche of Taoist, Buddhist and Confucian doctrines with a large helping of superstition mixed in for good measure. It was also an opportunity each year for Wu to have rice with his counterpart, Hun-yuan, from the Buddhist sangha. That is, he would have rice if it were before mid-day, for Hun-yuan's order demanded abstinence from food after the hour of noon. Wu smiled and shook his head to himself. But perhaps, he thought, our Taoist practices seem as strange to those outside the tradition. He looked forward to talking to his old friend once again, of debating the philosophical subtleties of their respective paths and enjoying a good laugh together; for although Hun-yuan was abstemious in much, he was, as a follower of the Ch'an (Zen) tradition, lavish with good cheer and laughter. Wu shook his head: poor Hun-yuan. How can a life of celibacy lead to enlightenment, when the sexual act is what most closely replicates the fire of celestial creativity?

Just as yin follows yang, however, Wu did not look forward to the visits of the Confucian officials with their superior poses, condescending attitudes toward the magical rituals and prying questions, always attempting to catch the monks, visiting shamans and artists, and pilgrims in some compromising situation. It was during this time that Wu made sure that there was no mention of the dual cultivation if the prudish Confucians were near. All offending text books, painted scrolls and sexual devices were safely hidden away. Even the library, which could not be closed to this intellectual elite, had to be self-censored by the monks. Dual cultivation classics such as Monkey, The Plain Girl's Secret Way and The Ancient Classic of Dragon and Tiger were routinely stored in a safe behind an innocent-looking panel in the event that a wave of Confucian fundamentalism would sweep through the government and result in raids and searches aimed at the always-suspect

Taoist community. It was no wonder so many Taoists chose to become "free and easy wanderers," working inconspicuously as herb gatherers or itinerant fishermen, rather than to settle permanently in either a village or hermitage, where their freedom-loving ways would be ever in danger of raising Confucian ire.

Of course, Wu realized that many critics berated the tradition for being too disciplined and restrictive, so (he shrugged to himself) it was best to answer only to the sublime Tao and not worry about the squabblings of one's neighbors. As for the Confucians, if only they could be more like their own sages and scholars, not only of antiquity, but even of recent times! In places, one could not tell the writings of the Confucians Lu Kun, Liu Wenmin and Wang Yangming from the realized masters of his own tradition. He was pleased, at least, that among the common people, such distinctions were irrelevant. They paid taxes to the Confucians, gave food to the Buddhists and made pilgrimages to White Crane Mountain, all the while keeping a shrine to some ancient god or goddess at the entrance to their house. As for the dual cultivation, while some might smirk behind his back, most accepted the strange ways of monks without too much curiosity. And for many women, it was an honorable way to earn merit and a small income to supplement their chickens and vegetable gardens.

Wu left Ming to himself for the first few days after his arrival, watching him from afar with concern and interest. He convened with Master Shan, and the two stood behind a screen in the library as Ming relaxed into a chair and casually unrolled several scrolls without reading more than a few characters on each, leaned forward, squinted and sat back again, this time gazing out a window at a patch of orange lilies stretching toward the sun. Wu motioned Shan to leave with him.

"My friend, I am concerned about Tu Ming's development," Wu said to Shan, who nodded agreement. "I feel he has lost too much essence in this initiation period."

"Perhaps," offered Shan, "the brothel has become debased. It may not be wise to continue to use its services."

Wu thought for a moment, then added, "No, I have confidence in Madame Chang. Generations of our tradition have received a good start there. Just the same, it would be wise to communicate to Madame Chang that she maintain several girls solely for this purpose, with no other patrons to distract them."

Shan, who was somewhat older but wirier than Wu, stopped to smell the honeysuckle which clung to the outside wall. The old men smiled at each other and continued on their way back to Wu's chamber.

"Will you propose a rigorous training period to restore Ming?" asked Shan.

"Yes, for another week. Of course, I must talk to him, tomorrow I think. However, I think it is important for Ming not to lose time in the cultivation practice he has started. I have a new partner in mind for him who will help him advance to the upper cinnabar field. It is important that he not be here during the relaxed, festive environment of the festival," said Wu. "That would be as dangerous at this delicate stage as to send him back to Madame Chang!"

*   *   *

Ming sat in his summer robe on the floor of the temple, facing the altar with its short candles and tall wooden statue of Wang Ch'ung-Yang, with an ironic smile on his cupid's bow lips. "The cause of desire lies in the mind," Wang had said. "Tame the heart, let not your imagination run wild. Look but do not see. Hear but do not listen."

It was no use. The great peace which had filled him during the days before he left Mei Cha had vanished. He tried to pull in his breath sharply and visualize the great pearl forming below his navel, growing, illuminating, beginning to move up through the central meridian. Then the nameless longing would return. Was it for Mei Cha, or for sexual consummation, or perhaps (the best case scenario) for the White Tiger Green Dragon, which was so completely different from sensuality. He needed to refocus. Perhaps he had not been reading enough! That thought would make the innkeeper laugh! But it was true, at least in part. The discipline of a lifetime had been shattered, his body was transformed and reconfigured, his heart was restless with energy which had no where to lodge. "As many times as you fail, refresh yourself and focus again," one of the sages wrote. "Like the Mysterious Female, your capacity to replenish yourself in meditation is infinitely renewable." He wondered who these sages were, and whether they really lived the practices they described! The hours dragged on. His nerves were frayed, his body twitched with discomfort and desire.

Wu smiled gently as he welcomed Ming into his chamber the next morning. There was a heavy mist on the mountain, clinging to their skin and clothing like a moist veil. The houseboy poured tea; Ming closed his eyes and steadily lifted the cup to his lips with both hands.

"How successful were you in self-control?" asked Wu as delicately as he knew how, a wrinkle of concern on his brow.

Ming opened his eyes, a bit red from poor sleep, and smiled back at his master. "I believe I have had an extraordinary introduction to this art," he said, bowing. "I thank you. But…"

"Yes?" urged Wu.

"But fear I am not making the transition back to monastic life so smoothly."

Wu watched him closely and said nothing for some time.

"The girl, Mei Cha," he said at last. "Did you love her?"

Ming looked surprised. "Oh, no, Master, not love," he said quickly, as though to disassociate himself with some crime. Then, reconsidering, he continued. "Not love. But affection, yes. I liked her very much."

"And you miss her now."

"Her, yes. But also our practice together." Wu said nothing. "Our practice…I suppose you would like to know the cycles, the details…"

"No, no," said Wu, brushing away the question, like a fly, with his hand. "As with your practice here, I get reports. I know what you are doing." Ming tried not to show surprise. How much would Wu know of his lapses into mere humanity?

"Do not fear," Wu continued, "that I will chide you for behaving like a man. This is to be expected, and, frankly, it would not be healthy or natural if you did not. At the same time, I fear the loss of essence has affected you deeply." He put his hands on Ming's temples and examined his bloodshot eyes. "Yes, you need a few days rest, some herbs, definitely more internal cultivation of the nonsexual variety with Master Shan. Then I have another partner for you."

This time Ming could not suppress his surprise. "Another partner! So soon?"

Wu nodded. "Yes, in village on the other side of the mountain. Su Ba is one of our most expert associates. She is a married woman who also has a business supplying medicinals to the local apothecary. Unlike these brothel flowers, which tend to wilt, she is a sturdy oak: strong, tireless and reliable. You will do well under her tutelage, but be prepared to work hard. This is why you must rest now." Ming rose and bowed. This was certainly not what he expected, but he was glad to have someone else set him on the path toward recuperation and the next stage in his cultivation. He would put thoughts of Mei Cha from his mind and instead, visualize the fair Su Ba, the better to be prepared for her lessons and demands on him in a few days time.

Chapter IV

▼

Wei Lu: The Tailpoint Accupoint

Duke Ai of Lu told this story: In Wei, there was an ugly man named Ai Ta'i-t'o. Yet despite his appearance, he was so highly regarded that the people around him never wanted to leave him. Young ladies of good birth told their parents that they wanted to become his mistress rather than marry gentlemen—there were at least 10 such cases reported! He wasn't a leader; in fact, he merely agreed with the majority and went along for the ride. He wasn't a ruler, so he couldn't save men's lives or fill their stomachs. To make matters worse, he was so grotesque that little children ran and hid behind their mother's skirts when they saw him near. And yet this ugly, bland, powerless man was sought out far and wide. What was the secret of this attraction?

I had to learn the answer, so I had him summoned to me. It was just as they said: a more hideous man I'd never seen! But he hadn't been with me a month before I started to realize just what kind of man he was. And after a year—well, I asked him to become my chief minister and put him in charge of the government! Before long, he disappeared, just like that! I was devastated and felt as though there wasn't anyone in the world I could share my rule with. What kind of a man was that?

*   *   *

The servant Yun clucked ominously to himself as the horse stopped where the path ended at the outskirts of the village. "You will be on your own now," he said to Tu Ming, looking nervously over his shoulder, his eyebrows drawn in as though to protect his face from some nameless evil. Ming had been riding without paying attention to the road, reciting in his mind the story of Duke Ai from the classic writings of Chuang Tzu. He opened his eyes, shook his head and looked around at the unfamiliar landscape. Then he saw Yun and was taken aback.

"What is wrong? You look as though you have seen spirits or wild beasts!"

Yun, who had been unnaturally quiet and circumspect during the day's ride, nervously untied Ming's possessions from the horse, his hands trembling. "I have heard about this place, but hoped it was not the place I had heard about!" he jabbered.

Ming slid down from the horse and put his hands of Yun's shoulders. "Whatever are you talking about? There," he pointed, "is a simple village. Here," he swept his arm, "is a road which ends and a cluster of modest houses with gardens and trees. That is all." Because it was dusk, Ming wondered if Yun's eyes had played tricks on him; or might it have been bad beer he had seen him swigging during his mid-day rice?

"Everyone knows about this place," he persisted, working quickly and looking about. "There is a witch here, I know it! I can smell it!"

Tu Ming turned so Yun would not see his smile. For all the confusion he had experienced in the past few weeks, he had begun to feel in control of himself again today. He was glad he had memorized the Chuang Tzu, with its wit, insight and stabilizing influence. But Yun: what would help him, except perhaps some chrysanthemum flower extract or a strong emetic!

"Master Wu assured me there were no witches here! And you must admit that Master Wu knows everything about the spirit world," Ming said, following the spirit if not the letter of the truth. "Here, take these coins and stop by an apothecary on your way back. Get something soothing and forget these games your imagination is playing on you!" Ming patted him on the back, secretly aware that Yun would find comfort in the arms of a harlot before he wasted good money on medicine! Yun finished his task, bowed nervously several times and led the horse rather quickly back into town.

Ming pulled a handkerchief from his sleeve and wiped his brow. It had been a warm day, and he sincerely hoped that the good housewife had a tub of water awaiting him. Witches! Spirits! Ghosts! Of course, they existed, but they clearly kept their distance from those who engaged in interior cultivation and refined their spirit. What a sad lot to be damned to a short life on this earth where the only pleasures were beer, a tough piece of meat and a dirty prostitute! No wonder Yun's imagination escaped to the realm of the fantastic.

The young monk carried his baggage gracefully a half mile through a grassy field before coming to the house, rather shabby, dark and large for a farm couple's, hidden among trees and rocks. There were no chickens running around the front, no farm animals visible. In fact, Ming wasn't sure if there was anyone there. He looked dubiously at the state of disrepair into which this once fine household had fallen.

Ming knocked several times on the shabby front door, then, sensing that he was being watched, glanced toward the window, where a rustle confirmed his suspicion. Suddenly, the door opened wide and there stood the most grotesque servant Ming had ever seen. So hideous was the woman that Ming wasn't sure whether it was in fact a woman at all, but perhaps a hermaphrodite, or a creature part human, part monster.

"Well?" she bellowed, nearly knocking him back with her powerful, deep voice. "What do we want with monks today!" She was a big-boned creature in a ragged brown shirt and pants, with a chamois skin hanging like a growth over one stooped shoulder. Her skin was tanned, like leather, with deep lines etched by decades of outdoor work. Her nose had been broken and was curiously bent in three places, sloping down to a twisted mouth with several visible stained teeth. She leaned on a bamboo broomstick, and Ming wondered if in fact Su Ba's servant was the very witch Yun feared.

"Good evening," said Ming, bowing, "I am Tu Ming from the White Crane…"

"Ah, Tu Ming, Tu Ming!" the creature smiled broadly and did seem to resemble a woman rather than a prodigy of nature as she relaxed into a more casual posture. "Ah, Tu Ming!" she said, drawing back and assessing the visitor from the top of his topknot to his shoulders, waist, legs and feet. "Yes, yes, a good specimen, Tu Ming!"

Ming blushed. "If it please you, I am here to see your mistress, Su Ba," he said uncomfortably.

The creature threw back her head and laughed. "Su Ba! Su Ba! You want to see Su Ba! And so you will," she said, pouncing with astonishing nimbleness to his side and grasping his arm with strong bony fingers. "For I am Su Ba!"

Ming's heart sank within him. Su Ba studied his face as he heard the news, and cackled merrily as she noted how he tried to conceal his confusion, horror and disgust.

"No, it's no joke, sonny!" she chirped, pushing him into the house, baggage still swinging from his shoulders. "That's the way they always look! I am surprised your monk friends never swap stories about me! But then it's not the White Crane I usually work with. Old Wu wouldn't blow my cover, would he? Not after all I've done for him and—well, a few of his charges over the years! Oh, sit here, sit here," she said, though it was so dark in the room it was impossible for eyes immersed in the summer sun all day to adjust so quickly. "Lu Wen! Lu Wen! " She lowered her voice, "I will have Lu Wen take your baggage, venerable young monk, and make us some tea so we can get to know each other better. Yes," she whispered, far too close to his face for comfort, "we are going to get to know each other very well indeed!"

Ming sat frozen in something approaching terror for some time while Su Ba made strange throaty noises and every now and then would spring to her feet and dance around him, eyeing what he hoped was his clothes but feared was the body she was imaging beneath them. "Hmm, hmmm!" she clucked, "he'll do, he'll do. Hmmm, did you have a good ride down the mountain? No rain, no rain! I do love a day like this," she rhapsodized, hopping to the window. She lit a lantern and scurried back as the tea arrived. "Good Lu Wen! Thank you Lu Wen! Hmmm…nice pale green tea and some sweet cakes too, for you, good monk."

Ming gratefully accepted the tea and, after Su Ba had taken the first slurp of her own bowl, lifted his eagerly to his lips and drank the entire cup, scalding his palate. "Oh, oh, not so fast, you must take care of your body," Su Ba said breathily. "You must not burn your mouth. We must make sure it is nice and healthy, hmm? Nice healthy lips, nice healthy mouth." She smacked her lips and swallowed two sweet cakes whole. "Hmmm?" she said, offering Ming some cakes. "No thank you," he said with some effort. Ming could barely breathe. All he could think was how desperately he envied and wished he could change places with the servant Yun.

                    *   *   *

Ming sat upright at the edge of his bed, his eyes frozen open at the candlelit space in front of him. Su Ban had ushered him to his room and told him he would have a good night's sleep thanks to the bags of herbs under his pillow. She had smiled broadly and crushed him in a bear hug which had been accompanied with little grunts of approbation. Then she told him where he could wash up and ordered Lu Wen to leave some bowls of cold rice and tea outside his room. "You rest tonight and tomorrow," she chirped. "Nice rest. Then we talk. Then we start to work!" She beamed at that last word. That was what bothered Ming. Whatever was Wu thinking of! There had to be some mistake. He would rather slide between the sheets with scorpions and snakes than with this hideous ogre who smelled of bitter ginseng and sesame oil!

Hardly had Ming fallen asleep at last when he was wakened by the chuckle of bamboo steaming trays and the smell of rancid pork grease. "Monk, monk!" The voice cut through a disturbing, early morning dream. Ming's neck ached from sleeping hard for a short period in an odd position.

Su Ba smiled as she scooped rice into bowls and poured water over the tightly curled tealeaves. "You want rice now, eh?" Hearing no reply, Su Ba sat down alone and ate both bowls with a hearty appetite. He was a fine-looking monk, but a little too refined, she thought. Probably paints those fancy watercolors of mountains and gorges like T'ao Ch'i without daring to put a dainty foot outside the cloister! She laughed and slapped a bag of roots against the wall dividing the two dissimilar housemates. Ming ignored the summons, slipping as he was into the morning t'ai ch'i routine, absorbed into the rhythms of its fluid dance. Su Ba washed down her meal with two bowls of tea and left some cold porridge and the half-full teapot by the door as she hopped off to haggle with a mercenary herb gatherer in the village.

Oddly enough (he noted later), his apprehensions and desire to remove himself from an intolerable situation led Ming to experience a powerful introspection. Sitting on the floor beneath a small window where a finch had built her nest, Ming felt once again the sense of poise, strength and weightlessness which once were a normal part of his meditation practice. The desire to remove himself from Su Ba's world opened for him a door to a deeper, interior awareness. Thoughts dropped away and soon he became one with the ch'i coursing through his body. Visualizing a ball of white light glowing in the lower tan tien, through concentration he lifted it up the center meridian to where it grew into a diffused light that flooded his being with profound peace and insight. He became fully integrated within himself and when he emerged as the sun approached mid-day, his good humor was restored and he was able to put his immediate travail in perspective, that of a flyspeck on the infinite sands of time.

Ming had gratefully discovered and sat down to eat the cold rice when the querulous sounds of Su Ba's and another, equally grating voice, reached his ears. There was a scuffle outside, some barrels overturned and rolled away, a pig—hidden previously he knew not where—squealed wildly and Su Ba cursed. Ming hurried out of the house to see the herb gatherer slink eagerly away, a defeated man.

"Five coins he wanted!" Su Ba spat, waving a ghastly lump of tree fungus. "He gets three—and this!" She beamed, shaking a switch in her other hand. The laugh that disturbed his already unsettling dream returned, the entire sturdy body of its owner shaking with glee; and a feeling of malaise began to sweep over Ming once again. When would his cultivation progress so that he was impervious to these changing tides? And to think Su Ba was the very agent supposed to assist him to achieve this immutability!

*   *   *

If nothing else, Su Ba was a capable administrator, Ming observed, as she outlined the work he would be expected to perform each day. "Chopping wood? I'm not so sure!" She squeezed his upper arm. "OK , but not like this!" she beamed, rolling back a shabby sleeve to reveal a well-exercised muscle. "You think you can work as well as woman, hmmm?"

"Let me tell you," she said later, as the day expired, "you are the sixth monk they send me!"

"The White Crane? I had no idea!" said Ming, who had changed into a clean brown robe.

"Not just. Two other monasteries—one pretty far. You know Bear's Paw Cliff Monastery?"

Ming had heard of it. In fact, it was one which had had some difficulties with the official censors some years before.

"My husband is often away," she continued. "He is not terribly pleased with my—arrangement—but agrees it must be done. He is a pious man! And talks to the gods all the time!" She tapped her head and lowered her voice, "Perhaps too much. For all that, he is gone a great deal with his business, and I am here with mine."

They were both quiet for some time. In the distance, the gong from a Buddhist temple signaled the evening rites. One bird sang its evening song as the sun dropped red behind the trees. Su Ba lit the lantern in the room.

"Come here," she said. "Sit." Ming put the broom he had been leaning on behind a cabinet and sank softly onto the pillow at Su Ba's feet. The lantern's light and the red glow of dusk agreed with Su Ba, who was transformed from an offensive ogre into a wise woman or crone.

"You are wondering what an old woman like me is doing as your teacher, hmmm? It is very mysterious, is it not! You study many years— five, six, how many?"

"Ten."

"Ten years! With the finest minds, with monks and masters from Peking…the big city! Then they send you to a two-bit whore…and then here, to an old woman with no teeth!" She laughed for several minutes at the idea. Ming was surprised that he was not embarrassed and in fact smiled back at her.

"Yes, it is hard to fathom," he admitted.

"Good! You tell truth!" She leaned close to him, smelling of gingerroot. "You know," she whispered, "I may be old enough to be your mother, but I am not as ancient as you think. I have not yet seen fifty summers like this, and hope, with the merit I earn working with young fellows like you! to see fifty more, like my grandmother. Can you tell an immortal by the clothes she wears?"

Ming was startled. In two days, he had not once thought of Su Ba as anything but a disgusting hag, until this moment. But the tradition of Taoism
was filled with crusty eccentrics just like her, wandering from town to town,
or disappearing into the mountains, or running a small business not far
from the village. Often, they deliberately adapted the mannerisms of the
marginally sane so as not to draw attention to themselves. Ming looked
deeply into Su Ba's merry, brown eyes and wondered if indeed he were in the
presence of a realized one such as the sages described.

"The dual cultivation, hmmm. It is not for everyone, you know. Your
master, Wu, thinks you are ready, eh? Well, we'll see! " She put both large
hands on his shoulders. "I have taken six monks through the Valley of the
Mysterious Female into the fire which burns illusion to dust. Five of these
have compounded the pill of the elixir which is beyond life and death—
the great dragon-tiger pill!" Her voice had become very soft. "Listen: there
is a poem, you may have learned it already! When man and woman come
together, it says, their feelings are merged, they are like clouds and rain.
They drink wine wantonly in a palace on the scarlet mountain and sleep
together, intoxicated, in the chamber of the purple climax. What does
their union result in? In one year they give birth to a child."

"I know the poem," said Ming, "but doesn't it suggest later on that the
dual cultivation is a symbol…"

Su Ba put her finger to her lips, closed her eyes and shook her head.
"No talk, no thought. Getting through to the spiritual embryo, is it an
idea…or a living experience? I tell you," she said opening her eyes wide,
eyes which now seemed very compassionate and loving, "throw out your
books, monk, and let your essence become aroused with life's desire.
Become intoxicated, feed on the boundless female energy and transform it
within yourself into the fertile seed of all knowing. If you doubt or resist,
you will lose it! But if you yield, all things will come to you."

*   *   *

Ming and Su Ba "swam in the silver river" for a week's time, pausing only for rest and nourishment. As long as he was able to ignore Su Ba's physical appearance, Ming's mind was delirious with ecstasy and, to his delight, he found that Su Ba's command of erotic technique (such as her knowledge of pressure points to block or divert the flow of essence) was so perfect that he was able to practice with her for hours without losing energy. With her guidance, his visualization of the golden moon became so intense that it seemed that the cool, lunar light was generated below the navel and rose like a living flame within. At the week's end, Su Ba was gone, having left a note that she was off to take care of her herbal business for a few day's time and to regenerate. She left with the occasional houseboy a list of chores for Ming to perform in her absence as well as specific instructions for continuing his cultivation alone. Ming was astonished how far he had progressed in so short a time; but soon missed the erstwhile ogre, the laughter which swung between extremes of the hideous and the sublime, and the carnal sensations which had vivified him for seven days and nights. Having ridden the dragon through the rainclouds and across the golden moon, he found himself in only a day's time sunk low, aching spiritually and physically, and wracked with a desperate sense of unfulfilling solitude. In the sometimes manic-depressive realm of the tiger and the dragon, the depressive element was conspicuously in the ascent.

Communication was swift and certain between the village and the White Crane, and since, unlike his initiation at The Yellow Bud, there had been no prohibition against attempting to contact Master Wu, Ming found consolation each night writing a short letter to his teacher, describing his progress and lamenting at his emotional relapse at Su Ba's departure. An example follows:

> Most venerable Master: In my solitude and discomfort,
> I think with longing of the White Crane and the simple
> life there I once knew. Perhaps, as you have often said in
> the past, summer's heat conspires to exacerbate

irregularities in the cauldron as well as those times when the internal fire flares sporadically, or dwindles to a barely lit ember. There is no doubt, of course, that your course of instruction has been a sound one, and I owe any wisdom and insight I may achieve entirely to your good judgment and care. The instructors you have appointed have been meticulous in their pedagogy; their practice has been sublimely illuminating. Nonetheless, I find that I am utterly dependent on their partnership to continue my cultivation. And how different their approaches!

As you predicted, my tutelage at The Yellow Bud primarily familiarized me with the varieties of sexual experience and provided an introduction to the yogas leading to immortality. There I explored with my partner the 10 all-healing positions, and she opened to me awareness of the 12 energy points rising like a snake along the spine. For the first time, I think I began to experience what the sages call the Valley Spirit, the Mysterious Female. This initiation prepared me for my current teacher, who is an astonishing master of the tantric kung fu. With her I have learned the truly infinite power of the female, at least as regards her reservoir of undefiled essence. Although I have had glimpses of the golden flower, still I see I have a long, perhaps painful period of practice and learning ahead of me before I achieve my goal.

While I had been prepared for the importance of self-control, I did not foresee, nor could you have warned me about, the depletion of spirit which would occur when disengaged from my instructors. The powerful forces of concentration which enable the dragon and tiger to copulate for hours shrivel into ennui and lassitude when the partner is gone for any period of time. In vain I sit beside my cot at night, candle-gazing, trying to "turn the wheel of the law," as we call our meditation on the revolving orbit of ch'i within the body. Eye-rolling exercise, swallowing the sweet nectar of my own saliva hundreds of times…these practices are stale and lifeless to me. My mind aches for my books, far more than those few scrolls I was able to bring with me; my heart craves the society of my co-renunciants at the White Crane; my body craves the very sublime exercise that exhausts while it energizes during this time when I sit at the feet of women—otherwise so ineffectual and insignificant in our society—and surrender myself absolutely to their creative power.

Worst of all, however, is the cloud of the black dragon which dims my inner light and oppresses my spirit. Can you assure me that this will lift, venerable one, and that one day I may transcend this mating dance to achieve immortality on my own terms (and with the help of no other)? Reassure me that this will be so, or I doubt I now can live apart from this dependency.

Physical labor provided what attempts at internal cultivation failed to supply: an outlet for Tu Ming's restlessness and an energy level which, undetected by him at present, had actually been augmented by his tantric practice. Lu Wen enjoyed a holiday and crept out with his fishing pole before dawn as Ming occupied himself with scrubbing, sweeping and weeding. Ming's pale, thin fingers chapped with unaccustomed labor; his once white throat grew hot and pink in the mid-summer sun. Each night, he stood in the clearing by the road, squinting in each direction for any sign of Su Ba before retiring to his room to face the barren alchemy of his stricken heart.

One night, not so many days after she first went into the hills to look for fresh talent among the herb gatherers, Su Ba appeared in Ming's doorway, rendered even more hideous by the harsh shadows of the lantern light, an enormous grin on her face. "Back, back!" she cackled as Ming startled from sleep, and then vanished as though to give credence to rumors about her magical powers. "Mistress Su Ba?" he asked into the night, but there was no reply. He returned to sleep, reassured that the odd normalcy of their previous week together would resume on the morrow.

*   *   *

Su Ba had roared with laughter at Ming's earnest pleas for her not to leave him, all the while avoiding looking directly at her weathered old face. "The old one has her uses, eh?" she noted with glee, pushing his shoulder rather too hard as she walked by to put away the day's haul of leaves and bark. Another week had passed with mixed success. It was one thing for Ming to have read about "gathering and lifting the fire;" it was quite another thing to lie in the semi-darkness with Su Ba and have her, through her extraordinary physical prowess, manipulate the subtle pressure points of his body and exert pressure with her own which enabled him to take the very generative fluids which could dissipate his spirit and instead compress and compact them, sending the sublime essence coursing up through the Yellow Hall and the Northern Sea (as the middle and upper cauldrons were sometimes called). She had laughed approvingly as his arms and legs thrashed involuntarily, and he seemed as though he would fly into the air or erupt into convulsions. It was as though the golden moon he had discovered in his sport with Mei Cha had become charged with liquid fire and refined into a higher level energy.

Tu Ming turned from Su Ba, a frown on his brow. For though his practice evolved to an amazing level of ecstatic activity, his questioning mind asked again and again, "For what purpose?" As the blockages within his psychic channel broke down, he experienced an unprecedented level of sensation. But as he had told Master Wu about sitting meditation, he knew that dazzling effects were dangerous, distracting practitioners from the Way. His question was not something he could ask Su Ba, who, for all her generosity, consideration of him and mastery of her art, was not intellectually equipped to deal with philosophical queries. She could barely read, and certainly had neither the training in nor affinity for logical debate and analysis.

Could his master provide an answer, or would he continue to remain so annoyingly evasive? He had stopped writing to Wu as his melancholia disappeared concurrent with his resumed practice. And though his body healed from his week's labors and returned to its original beauty and perfection, he felt that the outcome of his cultivation with Su Ba was only that: a matter of physical poise, a ballet of control and release, an inundation of celestial experiences of heat, energy and power. Enough for most men, surely, but somehow not for Ming. He felt farther from the Tao at this moment than when he meditated in the temple hall in all his unnatural, displaced celibacy.

"You think," said Su Ba in a serious tone which belied her smile, "that you control everything, eh? But the fireworks, they are not of your own doing, not yet, is it not so?" She put down her stock and sat beside him on a low bench. "You control less, eh? Your mind: it bolts wildly like a horse whose stall is on fire. Your body? Haven't you surrendered your control to me? Beautiful young monk and ugly old woman! Who would believe such a thing!" She exploded in a roar of laughter which had, however, no trace of mockery in it. "You used to be one…isn't being One your goal, monk? Now you are two and the lesser part of that two. You are dependent, but I have not made you so. Your own mind has tricked you.

"Don't fret: this is all part of the firing process," she whispered in his ear. "It is a stage in your instruction in the internal alchemy which men pass through when they are afraid to trust their original nature. You see, we mere, insignificant women, we hold the key to unlocking the cabinet where cinnabar, mercury and lead are stored. Your masters know this, but they will never say it. We have the formula for compounding the elixir. We know the method for balancing the five elements, earth, fire, wood, water and metal. We have the bellows for fanning the flame and precisely guiding it up the flue, into the chimney, out into the cold night air filled with stars and golden moonlight!

"Men seek the Immortal Fetus, but who has the combination to the lock of the secret of life? We who carry the source within our wombs and flow with the rhythms of the tides and the golden moon, we are the ones who are living knowledge. To you the female is 'mysterious,' the valley spirit remote and unknowable, a quest worth a lifetime of cultivation. But to us, the source of all being is clearly evident. It is our very self!"

Ming was drenched in perspiration, cornered by Su Ba, the oppressive humidity of the day, the walls of reason which closed in on him. "Don't faint, monk!" chirped Su Ba, giggling, as she poured a bowl of water and gave it to him to drink. "You still have rest to take. Save your heat for the firing process, hmmm? Come to me at midnight. You are ready for the Sixth Position of the Plain Girl. I will help you move your energy field to the kidneys and liver. Put yourself in my hands!"

Ming was no longer sure he wanted to put himself in her hands. There was no doubt that he had become addicted to the very sensory phenomena he knew could fatally distract earnest seekers from their goal. In fact, there was nothing imaginable he desired at that moment except to be with Su Ba and surrender himself to the firm hands which were like soft water rippling over smooth stones, the hard, aged body with its sinuous depths as fresh as spring moss. He knew the dangers involved in intercourse in which self-control was lost and energy dissipated, but was shocked to discover that the White Tiger, Green Dragon itself could enslave its practitioner, leading him to desire greater ecstasies and to forget about the Tao altogether. His mind rejected what his body and spirit craved. If only I could be certain that this was in fact a step leading to ultimate being: the thought roiled in his brain, teasing him out of sleep and spoiling his appetite for nourishment. If only I had reassurance from another—a master, another student of the dual cultivation—not having to rely on the words of this simple-minded enchantress (for, as Ming became more and more dependent on her art, he grew to regard Su Ba less as a friend and more as a captor).

The words of the sage flowed through his brain, reflecting his mood:
I alone am drifting, not knowing where I am.
Like a newborn babe before it learns to smile,
I am alone, without a place to go.
Others have more than they need, but I alone have nothing.
I am a fool. Oh, yes! I am confused.
Other men are clear and bright,
But I alone am dim and weak…
I drift like the waves of the sea,
without direction, like the restless wind.
Everyone else is busy,
But I alone am aimless and depressed.
I am different.
I am nourished by the Great Mother. (20)

And how did that passage begin? Give up learning, and put an end to your troubles! He smiled ruefully.

Her words about the Mysterious Female had wounded him deeply, for until he succumbed to her enchantments (for such he counted them now, which once were the sublimest art!), he had had no particular regard for the weaker sex. Now the words of Lao Tzu unfolded before him with new meaning: The female overcomes the male with stillness, lying low in stillness (61). And again: The Valley Spirit never dies; it is the woman, primal mother. Her gateway is the root of heaven and earth. It is like a veil barely seen. Use it; it will never fail. (6)

But how could he use it, which used him. "The Valley Spirit never dies," he murmured as he slipped in and out of sleep. Soon the heat within him became a fever, and his words delirious trembled on dry lips.

*   *   *

Ming's eyelids twitched. He felt miraculously cool, alive, though soaked under the light covering. Daylight stung his eyes and his nose burned at the pungent scent of camphor rising from damp batting on his chest. "It's broken, mistress! The monk is awake!" Lu Wen and the house-boy fluttered from the room like startled moths and went in search of Su Ba. Ming's mind was clear; he had no questions, thoughts, but inhaled fresh air like a hungry man eating chestnuts, swallowing them whole. He felt completely at peace with himself and his surroundings, though not yet able to move.

His eyes closed and when they opened next, Su Ba's own were mere inches away, dancing as always with delight. "Welcome back, monk!" she said, chuckling to herself. Her homely old face was a welcome sight. "Ah, monk, you are supposed to get strong with your cultivation, not sick. But no matter." She hopped back to the counter where a pan of hot herbs was simmering on a small burner. "This fever, it was good for you, eh? Your brain is calm, and you haven't been able to read! I think," she continued, bringing the foul-smelling brew to his lips, "that you lose more essence through here" (patting his tender scalp) "than here!" (gently pinching his groin)."

His skull cupped in her great hand, Ming sipped the hot liquid and tried not to think what lizards and snake eggs it contained. A witch? Yun had not been far off!

"But I have bad news for you, monk," she said, wiping his chin with a rag. "My husband is coming home. You must leave. Go! Back to your temple, back to the books which make you need to come here in the first place! In two days time, OK? You will be a new man, fresh as a baby by then." She paused and looked fondly at him. "Su Ba will miss this monk," she said, the same simple smile on her lips. "But you fight too much! All your teachers preach, 'Yield, yield!' and you dig down your hooves and rear back like an unbroken stallion. Why do you resist? Listen," she whispered, "to the voice of the female, who conquers by yielding, eh? In our cultivation, who was in control of the situation? Or 'What'! Hmmm?"

Ming didn't mind, didn't recoil from her arguments. He closed his eyes and tuned out, borne on the waves of tranquility which rose up with the fumes of his cup. It was good fortune that Su Ba was an apothecary. He wondered how she would manage her books when he left. He drifted into a refreshing sleep, filled with soft dreams.

Two days later, as predicted, Su Ba was surrounding Ming with a bear hug of farewell, fairly crushing the life out of him. She looked at her prodigee admiringly, almost coyly, a look such as she must have worn as a young girl learning the tantric arts. "You will be back, eh?" she said in comforting tones, though he was not in need of comforting. "Continue your practice! You do not need two. The dragon and tiger are here," she said, pushing on his chest. "Get rid of that blockage above the Jade Pillow," she said, pulling both his ears. Ming reddened with embarrassment as Yun appeared with the horse and fairly choked at the sight of monk and old woman in front of the house.

"See, Yun, there is no witch here, only this good lady," said Ming, as Yun took his bags, including a nice sack of fennel seed as a gift for Master Wu. Yun moved quickly so as to not dissolve in laughter at the thought of his own master copulating with a coarse old hen. Only a residual nervousness about the possibility of vengeful ghosts in the community kept him within the boundaries of prudent decorum.

"Yes, master, I have since heard many tales about this place," he sputtered. "Yes, I am sure I am quite safe here!" And at these words, he turned his back and guffawed into his sleeve, pretending it was a sneeze. Su Ba paid no attention whatsoever, focused entirely on Ming. A scrawny pig nuzzled her leg, which she swatted away with a stick.

"Yes," said Ming, sincerely, "I will return. I feel I can learn more from you now that my mind is clearer." His mind drifted to what kind of man her husband must be, whether he was a cultivator as well, or simply a hearty peasant hungry for the thousand pleasures Su Ba could no doubt provide to a man of the red dust.

When he turned from the horse, Su Ba was gone, as completely gone as anyone had ever been. He looked to the ground where the pig lay scratching its back. There was not even a footprint. "Looked for, she cannot be seen," the words repeated in his mind. The sky was brilliant blue, the humidity low and songbirds had not yet retreated from the rising sun. At a brisk clip, monk and servant, the one serene, the other edgy but bursting with tales for his drinking mates later that night, set out for the mountain.

▼

CHAPTER V

CHIA CHI, THE MIDDLE OF THE SPINE

Master Wu was surprised to hear that Ming was returning so soon, only a month after setting out and troubled to see the young monk as he peered through an obfuscating screen to observe him undetected. True, he was much more poised and confident than after his adventures at The Yellow Bud, but there was a worn, tired quality about him which was unsettling. Worse, his eyes darted back and forth, like an addict deprived of opium, and his skin was both sallow and streaked with brown, as though he had simultaneously spent too little and too much time in the sun. Wu watched closely. No, this time he had been careful to preserve his essence; Wu knew the signs. Ming's intellectualism, long his greatest obstacle to the True Knowledge, seemed to have been exacerbated by contact with the least intellectual of tantric masters! This was extremely puzzling. Wu decided to consult the I Ching and sent for his oracle.

Old Yan had performed divinations for Master Wu and his predecessor, Venerable Kung Mao, as long as anyone could remember. Crippled with arthritis and afflicted with a degenerative bone disease, he now was supported by the hermitage as an act of gratitude and charity, much as the owner of a prize racehorse might keep him on to an old age after he had long since ceased to be an economic asset. A grizzled but perpetually cheerful gnome, he was provided with a new suit of clothing every other New Year's. Wu reflected to himself that Old Yan might need a few months advance if he were to survive the fall and early winter in his current tattered habit.

With the personal set of yarrow stalks taken from Wu's own chamber, Old Yan set about lighting special candles in the hall, lit a heap of powdered incense and spread the yarrow stalks on a dingy mat reserved for this purpose. "Venerable sir," he smiled, bowing numerous times, "is there a particular question you would pose."

Wu closed his eyes and nodded. "Yes, it is about the next stage in the cultivation of my best student, Tu Ming. Advice, please."

The diviner bowed down to the sticks and manipulated them in a showy manner which belied his stiff fingers and wrists. Picking, and placing, and catching them between his fingers, he soon had the arrangement completed. "Sir, is there perhaps—you will forgive me for asking—possibly a lady involved?"

Wu, whose eyes had not opened, and therefore had missed Old Yan's special display which, ultimately, he performed only for himself, nodded again silently.

"Does the hexagram 'Return' suggest a reply, venerable?"

"And the secondary influence?"

"'Nurturance by the small,' beneficent master."

Wu opened his eyes. "Any moving lines?"

"I will say this: yin for the second place, good return, auspicious!"

Wu smiled. "I understand," he said. "Tell me if I am wrong." Old Yan grinned and bowed gleefully. It was a special joy for him to be so close to the mind of the great man. "'Entering and exiting, no harm will befall.

There is a companion: no fault! Reversing the path…going back yet going ahead!'"

"Excellent, excellent, venerable," squealed Old Yan. "Yes, this is a pattern of return which will lead to further development. It indicates that someone—your student perhaps?—has lost yang through yin. When the time is ripe—and only then!—the cycle will repeat itself and yang will rise again. Two moons: yin and yang. How can they come together without the new companion? This companion—she? I think so!—will come and restore his living potential. Reverse the false fire! Restore the real fire!"

Wu seemed satisfied. "And the 'Nurturance by the small.' Tell me what this suggests."

Old Yan looked down where he sat in an awkward, cross-legged position and stroked the stalks nearest to his twisted leg. "Only you can interpret this, master," he said simply. "'Make the small your food and drink. Submission subdues strength! Dense clouds do not rain…look to the Western province. Yin, clouds; yang, rain. Returning by the path, venerable."

"Isn't there a time element involved?" asked Wu.

"Seven days, master, seven days. "

Wu bowed and dismissed the oracle, who gracefully swept up the stalks in one hand and returned them to their brocaded pouch, returning his bow as he limped backwards out of the hall.

Wu paused a moment, reflecting on the reading. Then suddenly he clapped his hands and sent for Master Shan.

*   *   *

In an alcove off of the main temple, Ming and Li Feng sat in the candlelight with three coins. "I don't want to consult the official oracle," insisted Ming earnestly. "We can do this ourselves as we have for years."

Li Feng sighed. "But for something so important…"

"I'd rather not draw any attention," said Ming. "I have no doubt that Old Yan would find a way to get the message to Master Wu if I requested a reading. These coins will do fine. Do you have the scrolls? It's been so long, I am afraid that divination has not guided my steps as often as it should."

"You should rely more on this science!" Li Feng berated him. "You are too much of a poet! That is your trouble."

"Poet! It is my scientific rationalism which seems to work most against me! I must learn to become more spontaneous if I am to progress, like you. But when I try hardest to be spontaneous, just then it eludes me most dramatically."

Li Feng smiled. "Yes, and then you punish yourself by brooding about it!"

Ming shook his head in dismay mixed with self-deprecating humor, and tossed the coins six times.

"Hmph! That's an odd one," observed Li Feng, squinting back and forth between the coins on the floor and the manuscript in his hand. "'Treading': it means forward progress. Do you see the lake? It means the youngest daughter...harmonious, relaxed, joyful!"

"I see a tiger," said Ming, peering over his friend's book, "and a long striped tail I shouldn't tread on!" They both laughed. "Does it bite?"

"No, look. Treading the path completely, returning to the source. Consummate the beginning, complete the end! Very good, big brother! But do you know what this means regarding your own question?"

Ming sat back on his heels and looked relieved, but not decided. "I think it means that I must continue for an indefinite time. But the answer, when it comes, will be complete."

"'I think' indeed! Well, let's hope it's in both of our lifetimes!" teased his friend. Li Feng scooped up the coins and tucked them in his sleeve as the two monks went back to the refectory.

*   *   *

For Wu, the message of the yarrow stalks was preeminently clear. He would contact his old friend, General Kuan, about his daughter Chou Yin. Now there was an interesting case, just the sort of person to work with Ming during this difficult period. General Kuan had dedicated Chou Yin to study the dual cultivation five years earlier in her mid-adolescence. She had been a sickly child and he had made a vow that if she survived, she should either become a nun or otherwise earn merit and pay back his prayers by service to a monastic community. An artistic child who loved animals, Chou Yin chose to study the White Tiger, Green Dragon rather than leave the home and father she so loved. Although, as a Confucian official, the general had grave reservations about her request, he decided it was wiser to risk offending the court than the gods, so with utmost discretion (and he was in a position to buy discretion wherever it was needed!), he set about having her education expanded to include the sexual application of the internal alchemy.

Chou Yin, thought Wu, yes, obviously the correct choice. Exactly the sort of girl indicated by the oracle. Her refinements and good breeding would be more to Ming's style than the earthiness of Su Ba. He smiled to himself, though. Being a rougher sort, he had learned much from Su Ba and with far fewer traumas!

Ming's trouble, he mused, was that he was not only too intellectual, but also too open to suggestion when confronted by others who possessed inner power. And while he would not own up to it publicly, there was no doubt in Wu's mind which sex was superior. Was there ever any contest between nervous young monks ever on the verge of losing their very life essence, and the highly skilled wise women who were virtual reservoirs of ever-flowing energy? Even when women did lose a bit of their essence each month in menstruation, they seemed to come back even stronger for the respite. We try to create an imaginary embryo within us, he thought, shaking his head. When theirs' is the literal power of life and death!

     *   *   *

Wu let Ming settle back into the routine of monastic life for some time before taking him to the next step in his education. Ming had had time to reflect on what he had learned; after all, this wasn't a Ch'an monastery where shock techniques were used to break students out of constrictive mental patterns. Certainly, the breathing and visualization techniques Ming practiced during the dual cultivation blended beautifully with the classic meditation practices he had learned at the hermitage as a young man. The semi-regular routine of the hermitage with its astrologically determined hours for meditation and rice, study and exercise, had lulled him back into a state of mental and physical soundness. To this had been added new readings in the external and internal alchemies. Master Shan had begun a study group with Ming and six other monks around the core texts, most more than a thousand years old. The external alchemy dealt with the pharmaceutical and medicinal sciences designed to improve health and lead to immortality.

Master Shan insisted despite Ming's skepticism that immortality had in fact been achieved by the external alchemy. "When hermits and others vanish from our midst, what are we to think?" the old one asked. He told the story of the great Ko Hung who in the fifth century willed to die in the meditation position after a lifetime of meticulous cultivation and alchemical innovation. "Historical records show beyond a doubt that only his clothes remained in the coffin…he had escaped from the world of dust and flew to the land of immortals. How can you, with your scientific turn of mind, doubt the evidence which in this case and so many others is so apparent!" Ming countered that according to the reputable historical records he had read, the only outcome of extensive external alchemy was death by mercury or cinnabar poisoning, but Master Shan only laughed and indulged in a bit of paternalistic head-patting. "My boy, my boy," he chuckled, "that is exactly what the immortals want you to think!" To such reasoning there was no counterargument, so Ming decided to keep his research quietly to himself, and perhaps Li Feng.

The external alchemy, though considered a bit old-fashioned in recent centuries, was protected by court and temple alike from common curiosity, but was not as profoundly guarded from public scrutiny as the internal alchemy, not to mention its controversial cousin, White Tiger, Green Dragon. External and internal alchemy went hand-in-hand in the White Crane Hermitage, though the monks did not concentrate on producing a physical golden pill the way their predecessors had a millennium earlier. There was no serious effort expended on laboratories set up for refining the raw materials of nature (gold, cinnabar and mercury) into the living essence of the universe. Master Shan had no doubt that gold could be refined into cinnabar, the mineral "food" which provided the ultimate yang energy of nature ("To become nourished by cinnabar is to feast on the sun!" he once enthused), and cinnabar in turn could be sublimated into mercury, which in turn became a kind of gold by virtue of its capacity to gild other metals. The monks gossiped that Shan secretly kept a small furnace in a remote part of the hermitage where he continued his scientific experiments, eating little bits of bizarre metallic concoctions day after day in the hope of preserving his essence for all eternity.

"Cinnabar, the miraculous!" he would rhapsodize, to the concealed amusement of his students. "Unlike members of the plant kingdom, which are burnt and perish, cinnabar is heated into mercury then turns back into its own true nature once more."

"That is a beautiful metaphor," offered Ming.

"Metaphor! I do not want to hear about metaphors! That is for Buddhists, not for those who actively follow the path of the Tao," retorted Shan, offended. "Your modern writers—Liu I-Ming and others—have their heads full of metaphors and confuse young adepts with their talk of symbolism. What did Lao or Chuang need of metaphors? They spoke and lived the truth! See with your own eyes, hear with your own ears. I do not want to hear any more of these heresies against the Old Ones, these masters of obfuscation who mislead the young!"

Ming had not replied. In secret, he had discovered a copy of a manuscript by Liu I-Ming just that year and marveled over the scholarship and insight of one who could make sense of thousands of years of alchemical gibberish. But perhaps it was best to follow the teachings of the masters, not tread in potentially explosive territory, not at this time, when learning the dual cultivation as a means to enlightenment absorbed so much of his energy.

And so Ming and his fellows learned the Nine Cauldron method in theory if not in practice (and certainly not metaphorically!): each transmutation was carefully outlined in Ko Hung's masterpiece. The description of miraculous happenings as one proceeded with the nine steps of physical alchemy—the unleashing of red birds and phoenixes, jade maidens, gods and the ability of male adepts to beget children— reminded him of Patanjali's sutras, a Western text he had read in translation, as well as his own experiences in meditation (especially when hungry from fasting from grains). The hallucinations and visions were of the order that one was admonished to ignore and instead to focus on the highest goal. Weren't Ko Hung's descriptions of the Nine Cauldrons simply metaphors for these preliminary meditative states? Wasn't the Ninth Cauldron, Cold Cinnabar, flying without wings, a powerful symbol for union with the Void?

Master Shan would look down at Ming as though reading his mind, and slowly shake his head from side to side. "What is your worst enemy?" he would ask no one in particular, though Ming knew it was directed at him. "Your own mind!"

The internal alchemy was another matter altogether. To Ming, the process of stoking the furnace and nurturing the fire was both real and acceptably symbolic. In meditation as well as in his final cultivations with Mei Cha and Su Ba, he could feel the fire rising within him. It was authentic, there was no doubt about it. At the same time, the language of the internal alchemy—talk of furnaces, bellows, compounded pills—clearly was metaphoric, unless there was a miniature boiler room maintained by tiny firemen in each individual's belly! (And Ming would not have been surprised if Master Shan believed this to be true!) The internal alchemy used the language of the external alchemy to enable people to develop their inner power. The experience of great vitality, energy and insight was indeed similar to the feeling evoked by a billow of steam rising through a slue, or the controlled explosion of gunpowder. He could see that the dual cultivation, too, with the controlled flow of the semen back into the body, up into the Yellow Hall and the Northern Sea, was a combination of real physical change and symbolic representation of enlightenment. The expanded essence, rising like a phoenix, a red bird, feeding off the limitless female...no, this was not the time or place to dwell on such thoughts! Perhaps he was ready for another partner.

Indeed he was. And in a week's time he found himself standing with a letter of introduction at the imposing household of General Kuan, with license to ravish his daughter.

*   *   *

General Kuan, a weathered, stalwart warrior whose career teetered on the edge between acceptance and exile, looked sharply at Ming, but quickly assessed that he was a permissible match for Chou Yin. Ming sat at the feet of the imperious general in the main courtyard, surrounded by graceful vases, lacquered screens and female servants, some of whom were also concubines. It was a beautiful household, though not lavish; Ming sensed the tension which prevented Kuan from displaying the wealth his military expertise had brought him. His life was ruled by the whim of the court, and any display of excessive ostentation could be all that was needed to prompt the officials to dispatch someone with so much hidden knowledge, so many compromising secrets.

General Kuan did not entertain Ming for long, other than to ask him some curt questions about his role at the hermitage. He dismissed Ming shortly and sent him to the governess for tea, steamed dumplings and an introduction to his only daughter.

The governess was a heavily painted woman in her mid-40s, wearing an ornate brocaded gown of embroidered green silk. Her fingernails were long and curled, in the manner popular at court; her feet were tiny knobs, the so-called "golden lilies" produced by a lifetime of painful binding. Ming wondered if she had been the general's concubine before her beauty faded, or whether she was placed in the household after exhausting her usefulness at court.

The two sat in a small, intimate room across a handsome table with mother-of-pearl inlays. The distant sound of early autumn harvesting hummed in accompaniment to her (almost comically) lilting voice.

"I see you come highly recommended, Tu Ming," she said, pretending to read his introductory letters. "This is most satisfactory, since Chou Yin is a very special and highly sought after partner. She is not, however, particularly robust. And I know," she smiled broadly, without crinkling her painted eyes, "you will be most gentle with her precious body."

Ming bowed and lifted his tea cup as the governess did so. "I have been told that Chou Yin is a musician and artist. I have the greatest respect for the arts, and will cherish her as a partner in my cultivation," he said.

The governess looked coyly at Ming, playing with her fan. He certainly was a handsome fellow. What a waste, a monk's life! He could be the father of fine sons, a minister of the state…how his father must be disappointed! How many women he could satisfy, if only he did not have to follow this ridiculous regimen of sexual yoga!

"Very well," she said. "You may bathe now and tonight enjoy evening rice with the family. There you will meet Chou Yin. Tomorrow—unless she has one of her headaches—you and she will play the art of the bedchamber together." She moistened her lips. "I will be pleased to assist you…if she is indisposed." Ming gulped the last of the tea, bowed again and gratefully escaped with the houseboy. The air was sweet with jasmine; whether from tea, incense or his own imagination, he did not know.

*   *   *

Chou Yin sat to the side of the table with her lute. She squinted at the guest with interest. If only he would come closer! But then, they soon would be close enough. She listened to his voice as he was introduced. It was a pleasant voice, deep but soft, not sonorous. The voice of a poet, she decided, or a scholar. Perhaps someone with imagination. It always helped, imagination. Imagination for the adept who had to experience the initial rush of erotic knowledge only to visualize the course of ching flowing back against the currents of the natural order. Imagination for the female partner, who could use the dual cultivation to nourish her own ch'i or—worst case scenario—to daydream away the hours, to dream of melodies or poems in the shih form.

She turned the pegs, brushed the strings, sounding two or three notes—
before they had formed a melody, already the feeling came through
Each string seemed tense with it, each sound to hold a thought,
as though she were protesting a lifetime of wishes unfulfilled. (Watson 250)

General Kuan grunted in satisfaction, his hands folded on his full belly, his eyes half closed in bliss. Po Chu-I's *Song of the Lute* was a favorite, and invariably brought tears to eyes which had remained dry through death and devastation in his official duties. When Chou Yin played and sang this poignant song, his reserves melted. Yin sometimes thought what a secret it would have been for the enemy to know of this old melody and its effect on the Bronze Warrior!

Moved by these words of mine, she stood a long while,
then returned to her seat, tightened the strings, strings sounding swifter than ever,
crying, crying in pain, not like the earlier sound;
the whole company, listening again, forced back their tears.

And who among the company cried the most?
This marshal of Chiu-chiang, wetting his blue coat.

Ming listened thoughtfully and studied the face of Chou Yin. It was a young, fragile face, paler than his own, and not particularly attractive. Yin's teeth protruded somewhat, her shoulders were round, and there was sallowness to her complexion. But when she sang and played the lute, she was transformed into a creature of great beauty. Ming, too, closed his eyes and was transported in imagination back to the T'ang Dynasty and the heartbreak of two lovers who, once parted, would never meet again. Imagination: that is the quality that best describes her playing and her song. He smiled at Yin a smile she could not see, and wondered what their time together would reveal.

              *   *   *

"There is often confusion about the location of the furnace and the precious cauldron," said Chou Yin, as though to test him. "Where are these found?"

"The furnace and the precious cauldron are not together, as some suppose, in the lower Tan T'ien," replied Ming. "The furnace is below, the cauldron is above, here," he said, touching her forehead between her eyebrows. She cast her eyes down, as she had been trained to do, and then lifted them back clearly to his own and resumed her line of questioning.

"And is this an actual fire?"

"Surely, it is so! The yang fire rises at midnight. The yin convergence withdraws at noon. Yang fire in winter, yin convergence in summer: so it is written alike by scientists who study the alchemy of external nature and masters of the internal truth. "

"But how do you know it is actual fire?" she persisted.

"Through the actual heat one experiences as the furnace blazes, as the fire rises through the eight psychic channels and ascends at last to the cauldron in the original cavity of spirit."

"And have you experienced this fire?"

Ming gazed on Yin's smooth, open face so close to his. He admired her questioning mind and a mind too fine to be imprisoned in a female's form.

"I have." She raised an eyebrow. "But not, I fear, completely," he added. "One must turn the wheel many times before the cauldron boils."

"How does one turn this wheel? Is it an actual wheel?"

Ming laughed. "You know the answers to these questions. Must we persist!"

"We must," she said firmly, her hands folded primly on her lap. "Until I know the limits of your knowledge, I cannot help you rise to the next level of attainment."

"It is not a material wheel," he continued, pleased with her determination, "but a wheel of ch'i. It is the oval path which true vitality takes as it seeks to unite with eternal spirit."

It was Yin's turn to smile. "That is good," she said. "But what is this true vitality?"

"It is the generative force."

"Is it force only? Or does it have a material basis?"

"It is the golden elixir of procreation."

"Sperm? Sexual fluid?"

He was surprised by her candor, but nodded. "Yes, the same.

"And nothing else?"

Ming was annoyed. How much detail did she require? Why couldn't they simply undress and get on with it, without all this talk? But as he had the thought, Wu's criticisms of his excessive verbosity and speculation came back to him in a wave of sudden understanding. He blushed to realize he found in another the fault that was truly his own.

"The vital spirit, which is behind the golden elixir, that is what must be captured and circulated in the firing process."

"Force becomes elixir, elixir becomes force. It forms its own orbit, doesn't it?" she asked. He had no reply. It was a new idea to him and concerned him that he had not thought of the concept of a smaller orbit within the larger orbit previously.

For her part, Yin, however, was satisfied. He had the knowledge from books, some of the knowledge from experience, but was far from achieving his potential in the inner alchemy. She knew her own limitations and realized she could not bring him to the brink of ultimate awareness. That would be the task of future partners and would depend largely on the power and consistency of his own practice. But for now, it was clear which direction their cultivation would take, and she was confident that the results would be beneficial for both of them.

"Describe for me the larger orbit, the turning of the wheel," she said.

It was a basic question, and Ming felt a bit like a university student asked to recite rudimentary portions of the Confucian Analects memorized as a child. He was developing, however, considerable esteem for Yin's sharp mind and analytical questions. There was method in her approach, and he complied unquestioningly.

Ming describes the center of real vitality which lies within the body, 1-1/3 inches below the navel, approximately 2/3 of the way through the trunk. This golden furnace is the seat of life, both earthly and eternal, but, according to what Ming had been taught in his tradition, only comes into existence when the generative force is manifested through sexual arousal. At this time, the furnace begins the firing process. If leakage occurs through ejaculation or nocturnal emission, the fire is dampened and extinguished. The goal of every cultivator is to prevent leakage and turn the generative force, or light, around and direct it instead up the eight psychic channels through the middle and upper Tan T'ien and into the cauldron in the original cavity of spirit. This is done not by directing the flame directly up the sushumna (the hollow center of the spinal column) as in Indian kundalini yoga, but by a circuitous route which emulates the force/elixir/force loop which Yin described.

This process of turning the wheel, or light, around involves guiding generative heat up the back of the body beginning with the base of the spine. Essence rises through the four stages of ascent of the positive fire in the channel of control, reaches the crown of the head, then glides back down the front of the body as the descent of negative fire in the channel of function. It was all so clinical, Ming thought, like dissecting a grain of rice to discover the mystery of nourishment! He recalled his most sublime cultivations with Su Ba and felt for a moment the generative fire stir within him.

"Concentrate!" berated Yin gently. "First I must know the level of your understanding."

"But isn't action the point of our cultivation?" retorted Ming, leaning forward, partly to emphasize his concern, partly to dissipate his own accumulating generative energies.

Yin smiled softly and touched his hand. "Understanding is a convergence of knowledge and experience," she said. "One relies and feeds off the other. Just as we would not interrupt our practice to go read books or discuss each other's alchemical history, so we should not abort this critical review to initiate an incomplete experiment in cultivation."

Ming shifted on his cushion. "You said our. May I interrupt and ask what you meant by that?"

Yin released his hand, lowered her eyes in the stylized manner she had been taught and raised her amber eyes to his again. "You are, perhaps, under the impression that it is only your cultivation that we develop here?" There was a gentle, almost mocking tone to her voice.

Ming did not know what to say.

"Go ahead. Tell me, Tu Ming, what is the role of women in this practice?"

"Why, to provide their male partners with the infinite essence of the female to increase his longevity and achieve ultimate realization of the Tao. The female partner, in turn, gains merit for her sacrifice, which is not so great because of her great store of essence. Of course, I have heard of female adepts nourishing their ch'i...but...surely you can't seriously suggest..."

"Yes, I do suggest, and your Master Wu will support me in this. Our practice, Tu Ming, is the dual cultivation. Dual means two. Not only will you benefit, but I too will develop as I seek to live in harmony with the Tao, bring an end to my debilitating headaches, nurture my visions, experience a higher state of consciousness."

"But that is for nuns!"

"Then that is what I am. You have studied with a skilled courtesan and an apothecary-practitioner. Now you are studying with a nun, though, granted, one who still lives in the service of her protective father. But that could end at any time, given political uncertainties. At such a time, I am prepared to enter the Abode of the Celestial Maiden beyond the Wei Valley and join my sisters in cultivation and healing. Through our cultivation, both you and I will develop our abilities to generate heat and send it coursing through our bodies like shooting stars or displays of fireworks bursting over and over again in the night sky. "

Ming sat some moments, at a loss for words. He felt that he had a higher regard for women than many monks, who joked about using up female sexual energy as though the "donors" barely qualified as human beings. "But, surely, you do not plan to rob my own limited store of essence for your own development!" he said at last.

Yin smiled and patted his hand gently, tilting her head coyly to one side. "No, what we will enact will only build your store—and mine! Each of us, singly and together, like the great t'ai ch'i, will compound in the cauldron the seed of our own spiritual child. But I cannot take you any further than that. Then it will be up to your master to direct your development with others who are more highly attained."

At Yin's request, Ming resumed his description of turning the wheel of essence. As he described the various phases and points, he felt the small hair at the back of his neck stand on end as the essence rose up, and the fine down on his stomach tingle as he described its descent back into the pit of the furnace. Over and over again, nine, 64, 144 times, the wheel would turn. But in the back of his mind, was this new thought: a partner who was not simply a servant to his need; a partner who developed as he did. It was fantasy, pure imagination! It was sensible, a logical and desirable union. The two thoughts flipped back and forth like an undertow as he described the sexual activities which supported the firing process, and felt himself grow very warm despite the coolness of early fall.

"And what of the golden elixir of your tongue?" she asked, herself as cool as the chrysanthemums beside her chaise.

"I have studied this with Master Shan," he said, "and have mostly concentrated on the control of this fluid in private meditation."

"Tell me what you know."

Ming described the two channels under the tongue where the springs of the upper golden elixir converge and flow and the techniques which direct it to the channel of function, drawing it into the furnace where it joins the lower golden elixir in the production of heat.

"Do not lose saliva by swallowing it needlessly," cautioned Yin. "Do you know singly how to increase the flow and channel it into the cavity of vitality? In the dual cultivation, in turn, one partner gently touches the palate of the other with the tongue, releasing this nutritive nectar and guiding it into the lower tan t'ien. This is a certain way to strengthen your blood!

"But we have had enough of this discussion," she said at last. She could see he was on the edge of an unstable balance of arousal, fatigue and confusion. It was a good blend for her, as the controlling partner, to initiate a preliminary round of White Tiger, Green Dragon.

"It is early, yet I see you are tired. Yet, I detect the arisal of the clear." She took his hand and led him into the adjoining room, which was filled with the scent of dried lilies, sweet wood and the skin of small oranges. It was a luxurious room, with no windows, but a ventilation duct to allow for a small stove or candle. Yin lighted a lantern and closed the door behind them. Her hand ran lightly over the strings of her lute, left standing near the light. The other hand swept softly to her hair; she plucked out the sharp tortoiseshell pin which held her chignon in place, releasing a rill of dark hair. Ming was relieved as she placed the pin on a table and turned away; he had heard that many female adepts used such pins as acupuncture needles to stop the loss of essence in male partners! Yin faced Ming as she let her brocaded robe fall in one sensuous rush from her naked body and, pressing close to him, lifted her broad lips to his own. He wrapped his arms around her in an instinctive gesture of protection, warmth and a desire he must allow to go only so far, and sank gratefully with her into a bed of silk down bunting.

*   *   *

Cultivation with Chou Yin was entirely different from Ming's experiences with his previous consorts. Yin was no courtesan, like Cha, and not an acrobatic technician like Su Ba. Her focus clearly was on the union of two, the yin and the yang, the White Tiger and the Green Dragon, and in this, their practice seemed to him at this moment more perfect, a step beyond the initiations he had experienced with mixed results. For every nurturing movement Yin yielded, there was one in which she drew some gift of the body and spirit out of him. Yet the development of the inner fire proceeded, growing ever warmer. "Think of the bellows," she whispered to him during one of their couplings in which she sensed his questioning mind had interfered with their practice. "The bellows blows out the air, then sucks it back again. It is an alternation between taking in and giving out, a rhythm, a flow. Do not think that I will ever deplete your vitality…it will never happen! Nor can you imagine, if it even would occur to you, that you can exhaust my spirit. The fire within our bellies is one fire. Let it rise in perfect unity both within and between us."

Ming had smiled into her soft hair and focused every cell of his being on the firing process. The heat between and within them was intense, and, in the sixth cultivation, he felt the fire rush up his back and circle down through his nose to his groin, as though he were charged with lightning. Feeling this movement within him, it was Chou Yin's turn to smile to herself with pleasure that he had learned how to the turn the wheel, something she had been experiencing for herself since their second night together.

But all was not well with Chou Yin, who continued to be wracked by debilitating headaches several days a week, with a severe attack every two weeks. During this time, she was unable to see Ming, and remained secluded with her maid servant, unable to eat or drink anything except a weak medicinal tea, her skin clammy and even paler, if possible, than in its natural state. During these times, she had visions of the tai chi and the turning wheel, glittering, flashing and dancing before her eyes, whether they were open or closed. Because of this, the servants were in awe of Chou Yin and a little afraid as she retreated to the darkness of the household temple to wait out the passing of her pain.

Because of these interruptions, Ming's cultivation was not conducted predictably, night after night, though it did follow a schedule dictated by the regularity of Yin's attacks. Once he had experienced "the round fire that has no end," however, he was able with practice to replicate the process, if not the intensity. Many nights after dining with the general and his entourage, he would retire to his chamber and visualize his cultivation with Yin sensation by sensation, step by step, until the circuit was completed over and over again. As long as he was able to keep his questioning mind at bay, the practice nourished and sustained him, and would be replenished once or twice a week by his teacher and tantric partner.

Ming was concerned, however, that she seemed to lose even more weight, and sometimes was too weak to cultivate beyond an hour. He noticed, too, that there were no new paintings in her portfolio and her performances at dinner became fewer until they stopped altogether. The servants talked of enchantment, and began to stare reproachfully at Ming, as though he were in fact the demon who sapped their mistress' strength. And certainly, from his perspective, there appeared to be a correlation. As his practice improved and his mental and bodily health flourished, his partner waned, withdrew and faltered.

One day before the winter plum had blossomed, Ming received an urgent message from Master Wu to return to the hermitage immediately, with no explanation or reason. He gathered his belongings in a satchel and went in search of Chou Yin, but could not find her. The servants were remote and uncommunicative. He went to the household temple, hoping to find her there, but she was nowhere to be seen, even as his eyes accustomed themselves to darkness and candlelight. He returned to the main house and asked to see the general; he, too, was gone, and his personal secretary told Ming through a servant that he could not see him this day. A rickshaw waited outside the courtyard. Ming was hurried into the seat and respectfully, but hastily, dispatched.

As the rickshaw rattled along the road out of town, Ming twisted around, looking back with consternation, confusion and a mounting sense of alarm. But soon the general's estate was no more to be seen, a light shower of snow began to fall as day slipped into evening, and the flat countryside began to slope upward toward White Crane Mountain.

* * *

"Three partners, three lessons. What are they?"

Wu looked kindly at the forlorn monk beside him. Perhaps Ming was one of those contemplatives who must seek through the mind. But isn't it the role of the master to challenge the student and turn his mind around, that seeing reality in a new and unfamiliar light, he may be more likely to recognize it?

"This is no test," Wu reassured him, resting his hand on the young man's shoulder. In fact, they sat informally after midday rice, while Master Shan and most of the other monks and students were at a martial arts festival in the village. The refectory was cold and empty except for these two, several other small groups of much older monks and a number of servants, all of whom left master and favorite student a respectful distance apart.

Ming did not have an immediate reply. Wu waited patiently for the complicated intelligence to sort through the knowledge and experiences of the past nine months. Then he said, "Do not worry about parallels of practice to learning. Think of your first initiation, at The Yellow Bud. In a word or two, what did you bring back?"

"Beauty," said Ming immediately. "A sense of aesthetics."

"And from Su Ba?"

"Patience!" (Wu tried to conceal a smile) "Tolerance and respect."

"Very good! And what of this last adventure?"

Ming's glance fell. "Confusion, apprehension..."

"You mean about the girl's condition? No, no, do not worry about that! And do not look at me so reproachfully. The girl is not well, but in no great danger." Ming started and looked up eagerly for more information. "No, she is no longer part of your life, no more so than the young prostitute and the old apothecary. Yes, yes, she will be well: she needs rest. And she will play the lute and sing again, do not fret. Though it is best, as you can understand, that in your consciousness she dies a natural death! This is part of the problem, you see. You must not be attached to these vessels, whose only purpose is to nourish your essence and lead you to immortality!"

Ming set his lips firmly together and looked away. "I do not believe these women are vessels," he said. "And Chou Yin," he turned to Wu, "above the others, is an adept in her own right."

"And superior to you, I have no doubt!" Wu replied, his eyes narrowing with mischief. "Yes, yes, tell me, then, what words describe your most recent level of cultivation."

"Empathy, humility. Certainly, sharing."

Wu nodded and drew his padded robe closer across his chest. "Those are worthy values. Yes, you make progress, my son, but are still far from the goal."

"The goal!" Ming bristled, then recoiled. "I no longer know what the goal may be. In this world of dust, in which we spend but a few short years and which are so full of hardship for so many, what is the point of achieving individual liberation while so many thousands consider themselves fortunate to have a cup of rice, when even in peacetime one is at the mercy of an omnipotent state!"

"My son," said Wu, "you sound more like a Buddhist every day! But wait. Think of all you have read and studied, what you have experienced in your practice here and with these helpful spirits. Focus on the internal reality—the inner alchemy—where the very seed of life is released, planted and grows. Stay in touch with this source, my son, and it will lead you, as it well-nigh has on several occasions, to the irrefutable answer which cannot be expressed in words. That is the very best we can hope for and cannot hope to muffle the noise and clamor of the day to day."

But it was not noise and clamor merely, thought Ming, too moved to speak. His concern and regard for Chou Yin had opened up a wellspring of compassion for all beings just at a time when he was instructed to withdraw into himself and focus on the circulation of his own chi.

Wu knew his thoughts, and patted him consolingly on the back as he rose to return to his chamber. "Compassion is the noblest sentiment," he said in parting. "Its fulfillment is complete within your individual practice!"

Five days later, Ming received a message from Master Wu. It contained the name of a niece of a Tibetan princess in exile and instructions to go with Yun the first day after the new moon. "Consider this next stage in your cultivation a prescription to improve your spirit!" wrote Wu. Ming read the message several times, unable to fathom the master's words.

CHAPTER VI

▼

YU CHEN, THE BASE OF THE SKULL

It seemed as though Ming had been transported in his sleep to Mnon-sum, the Tibetan settlement halfway between the White Crane and the Chinese border. Had he been lost in meditation or simply asleep or perhaps drugged? Ming could not be sure. A kind of amnesia hung over his mind, disorienting him as he squinted into the setting sun and looked out of the sheltered cart in which he rode. He could not remember the name of the servant who was reining the mule outside what must have been an inn, but certainly of no kind Ming had ever seen before. It loomed between him and sunset, filled with shadows and stone, dark and edged in ice. The servant hurried into the shadows. Ming shivered, his forehead burned and there was an uncustomary pounding in his head. He withdrew back into the warmth of the cart, with its hay and thick blankets. As though answering his thoughts, the servant, who was named Dran-sron, soon reappeared, with a covered bowl of hot tea in a quilted basket.

"I asked for Chinese tea," he said, bowing and smiling broadly. Ming accepted the bowl with a nod. What else would he ask for, Ming thought morosely as the servant disappeared. Ming pulled the thick curtain tight against the cold evening air. Traveling, he reflected, sipping the hot, acrid brew, did not agree with him. Wouldn't he have progressed further if he stayed in his monastery, meditating in tranquility? With each adventure he seemed to lose his sense of certainty and assuredness. His command of the sexual arts increased in inverse proportion to the development of his spiritual powers, at least short-term. Certainly, there were peak moments of insight and ecstasy in the midst of the act; more often, there was the embarrassment of ignorance unmasked, of learning from someone outside of his tradition. Admit it, he challenged himself with a wince: of learning from women! He shook his head vigorously and gulped the tea with intense gratitude, feeling strength flowing back into his body like a blush.

Yet, Master Shan had said we learn from all nature: from the slave as well as the master, from the mouse as often as the lion. Sexual learning was different, of course. It revealed the inner core of one's being, the place where the Mother of all things created the seed of life out of herself. In the White Tiger Green Dragon, we entered the origin of who we are. We are stripped naked and given over to the other, and, if we are wise and skillful enough, can channel the energy of the Tao itself into the seat of all realization and perception, the human mind. Then why, he asked himself, reaching for his monk's robe and boots, do I feel at this moment so far from the goal? He shuddered, and placed the empty bowl beside him.

It was a question which remained in his mind throughout the night, as he lay awake, listening for an answer which would not come. He felt unnaturally alert lying on the unfamiliar bedsack, sweet with husks and resins he could not name. Was he fated to wander from partner to partner the rest of his days (which, at this rate, would not be long!), achieving each time a little more synthesis between body, mind and spirit, drawing ever so slightly closer to the Tao, only to withdraw and gradually lose it all again. And what of these partners? Did they remember him after he had gone, or was he too just an instrument of their own realization? Had he used them for his own development at the peril of their own souls? At one extreme, he had read that Taoist monks were no better than vampires or rapists, perhaps worse, for they plundered the very life essence of their female partners, many of whom were sold like slaves into practice of the dual cultivation, or who chose it as a last resort against starvation or abuse at the hands of less spiritually inclined men. Master Wu had cautioned him not to think of the personalities of his partners, but each had disclosed to him not only a new level of the firing process, but also a rich and interesting personality. If it could be said that he was the parent of this spiritual embryo which struggled to survive, then each was for him a co-progenitor. As he drifted in and out of an unrefreshing sleep, Ming saw their faces and bodies swimming in and out of his consciousness, like wisps of incense filling the room with their perfume.

Dran-sron watched the young monk sleeping as the sun rose in an orange cloud to the east. Like most of the Tibetan expatriates living in Mnonsum, Dran-sron was not what he seemed. Circumstances dictated that he earn his rice in China, so work he did, though not in the scholarly manner he would have pursued in Llasa. The work was agreeable, however, and he was grateful to be in the favor of several monasteries and convents where a servant fluent in Tibetan could be useful. One never knew what would happen politically; it was good to do honest, needed work and be rewarded for it. This monk, though, was different, and concerned the usually smiling Buddhist. Taoist monks should be merry! Especially, he thought wryly with a half-smile, those fortunate enough to have the cream of the nation's daughters as their sexual intimates. Dran-sron had been a Yellow Cap himself, at one time, celibate and wary of women in general. That had changed once he found himself in need of rice and a place to sleep in a foreign land. He thought fondly of the widow and her daughters who took him in and introduced him to the monastery as a place to work and serve. It was from Li Chi that he first learned of the dual cultivation and escaped from the karma of his own inhibitions. So much had happened since then! But now was not the time to dwell on his own past. The young monk was troubled. Perhaps the princess would be just the person to raise his spirit, to rekindle his desire for the knowledge that cannot be attained by mind and spirit alone. He placed his hand on Ming's shoulder and shook him gently. Ming woke irritably, then, sensing his own rudeness, nodded to Dran-sron, accepting the morning bowl. Dran-sron left quickly, and Ming arose, stretching his lean muscles like a cat. He went outside to relieve himself, and returned with delight to the comparatively warm room and hot tea. Plain Chinese tea, nothing remarkable: what did Dran-sron mean last night, he wondered. Perhaps the barbaric Tibetans were accustomed to stewing ginkos in their brew, like certain herbalists! No matter. Ming breathed deeply and settled into a round of cleansing breaths. In the saffron light, he shone, like one of Dran-sron's ruddy countrymen.

*   *   *

Dran-sron bowed and, with an expression of hope and tenderness which Ming could not interpret, left the young monk at the temple's door. It was an overcast day, threatening snow. Ming entered the large, squat building quickly, pushing the massive door closed behind him with all his body's weight.

The hall was dark, with a heavy, unfamiliar scent—like tar mixed with incense and perhaps rancid fat—hung in the air. Lanterns illuminated the walls on which monumental frescoes of demons and multi-armed bodhisattvas loomed, rendered not quite so ferocious by the dim light. The ceiling was much higher than he would have thought when viewing it from outside. As his eye glided over the walls around him and became accustomed to the darkness, Ming began to notice a number of ledges, nooks, grottoes, in which foreign statuary forms—tigers, goddesses— perched or crouched, poised for all eternity in the cusp of a pounce. A chill swept over Ming's body. The silence, except for the occasional gutter of a candle, had a presence and life all to itself, as though it were a huge, disembodied soul pressing down on an unbeliever.

There was nothing to do but wait. Ming looked around on all sides once more, then walked to the center of the temple, where he gracefully collapsed into the lotus position, took a deep breath and began to slow his pulse in preparation for a light meditation practice to make good use of the time. He breathed slowly and deliberately. The silence with its sticky, spoiled scent pressed against him. Ming did not resist. The pressure became an embrace. The silence seemed to grow, obscuring the sound of his own beating heart. He felt calm and at peace.

The scream, when it came, ripped through him like a flaming spear. It hurled out of the walls, lightning-swift and shrill, with overtones like little arrows shooting into him from all directions. Ming gasped, eyes bulged wide, his chest heaving wildly. Shooting down from one of the high ledges, the thing landed on its haunches 10 feet before him in a trail of twisting serpents flailed out on all sides, its face a mangle of deformity, gleaming with matted blood. Clouds of the foul-smelling odor rolled toward him and stung his eyes as he looked frantically for a place to hide quickly in the large empty hall.

The thing leapt into the air and somersaulted three times, until exactly in front of the trembling monk. "So!" it exclaimed, jumping to its feet and ripping off its head. "You must be the monk they told me about!" And, beneath the false head, was the broad grinning face of a young woman. She kicked aside the cloth banners which looked so much like snakes a moment earlier and tapped his leg with her booted toe. She straightened her smart magenta pants and blue-green tunic, adjusted her sash with its elaborate red and gold embroidery, and shook a shock of black hair, escaped from a bun, out of her eye. "Ugh…I'm getting too old for that! Well," she said, extending a hand and pulling him up, "get up, then, don't just sit there. We have much to do. Yes, yes, I am Lekshe Tsogyel." She pulled a particularly wicked-looking pin—long and iridescent—from her hair with a flourish, unleashing a magnificent tangle of hair over her shoulders. Bending over, she half-whispered slowly, "Welcome to my temple, monk. You have much to learn of…courage!" she barked the last word, causing him to flinch, not yet recovered from his original fright. "Well," she said, turning around and walking over to the incense pot she'd left on the floor behind her, "I have been looking forward to your visit." She stretched her arms over her head and swirled to face the main altar. "There is absolutely no one to talk with here!" she yelled, her powerful voice reverberating among the stone tigers and Black Taras around her.

Ming looked within to tame his unsettled nerves. The embrace of silence had been replaced by a peal of laughter, which rang like a chorus of golden bells within his skull. Ming decided he liked this creature and, as his heartbeat returned to normal, slid into a smile of contentment and opened his liquid eyes. Lekshe looked over her shoulder just then, and saw them sparkle in the candlelight. "So!" she said again, much softer. "You are not such a sheep." She clapped her hands loudly three times, and, for effect, did a series of cartwheels across the hall to the far wall. "This is mine," she said, landing perfectly on her feet and waving her trailing garment about to indicate the entire space. "My uncle, a remarkable lama in Llasa—gave me charge of it. And also to keep me out of his hair!" She laughed again, a strange, musical laugh to Ming's ears. He noticed the ceremonial sword at her hip, which she patted as she spoke. He wondered if she had received that from her uncle as well. She is so clean, he thought. Not at all what I had expected from a barbarian from the West!

"Well?" she chided. "Aren't you going to rise? Or at least if you are to remain on the floor, then please perform a hundred prostrations in my honor!" Ming rose slowly on his still shaky legs and blinked several times: no, she did not disappear. Not a hungry ghost after his soul, nor a fox spirit eager to devour his essence. It was no hallucination brought on by travel or fatigue. He shuddered, and realized he was drenched in sweat. But this—how could it possibly be? How could this be the princess Lekshe Tsogyel?

The spirit flipped at a leisurely pace four times, feet over hands, in his direction. "I hear you're quite a scholar," she said as she landed neatly on her knees before him and accepted his hand with pleasure as she rose. "Well, we'll see, won't we! " She winked and patted her sword, cocking her head to one side. "Come!" Nearly as tall as he, she swung an arm over his shoulder. "I have humble rooms on the other side of the Great Mala," she pointed to a painting on the opposite wall, "where we can talk about the stars and alchemy and Ancestor Lu. And have some nice, hot tea, would you like that?"

The servant summoned by the three claps emerged from the shadows and bowed in their direction. Lekshe Tsogyel grabbed Ming's hand and ran, with him straggling behind, toward the direction of a crack of light in the wall.

The caretakers' rooms where Lekshe lived were anything but humble. In fact, Ming thought they were as well appointed as the best Buddhist temples he had ever seen, though somewhat more gaily decorated. Instead of mandalas depicting the terrors of hell, colorful thangkas hung from the walls providing insulation, protection from the harsh acoustics of the main temple and visual stimulation. They were, on closer inspection, quite stimulating. For each hanging depicted divine beings in the ecstatic throes of sexual union.

Above the thangkas were high windows which seemed to shower the room with light. The sickening smell of the temple was replaced with the odor of oranges and sweet spices. There was a sense of coziness about the place, with its randomly scattered rugs, blankets and assorted odd bits of furniture and knickknacks, which appealed to Ming and was unlike anything he had experienced before. Lekshe curled into a corner of a large divan and, with an ornate hand gesture, indicated Ming should join her at the other end. She pulled a striped purple throw over her legs and threw her head back against a cushion. Ming's eye went from Lekshe to one of the thangkas and back to her again. Yes, she could double for the dakini depicted there! And was her knowledge of the tantric arts as exhaustive?

"Tea, yes, delicious tea!" she piped up as the servant brought in a tray. She said something to him in Tibetan, causing the bent old man to squint at Ming with sadness and shake his head. "He does not understand," said Lekshe taking a few noisy sips of the brew, "how you can stand it without yak butter!"

"Yak butter!" exclaimed Ming, holding the cup away and looking down contemptuously.

"No, silly monk, there's none in yours!" she laughed. "I told him to prepare some of that horrid, insipid brew you Chinese are so fond of! I, on the other hand, am enjoying this nourishing Tibetan food!" She showed him her cup, with its cap of floating fat, and he made a deliberately sour face which caused her to burst into laughter again. "Yes, " she said, "you see, we Tibetans are compassionate. Something you Taoists could learn much about!"

Ming pretended not to notice a remark which stung. To his Chinese sensibilities, it was a rude remark, not a joke, though the ruddy-cheeked woman seemed to think it was the soul of wit. "You will get used to me," she said, digging into his calf with her toe. "Just you wait!"

Lekshe sank back a little further and regarded Ming silently for some time. He was not quite what she had expected, to be truthful. Among the lore she had devoured as a student hungry for knowledge were endless lives of Taoist sages—Master Wang, for example, and the female sage Su Pu-erh. Their lives were so colorful, extraordinary! Feats of levitation, riding on the backs of dragons into the swirling clouds, conjuring spirits from toadstools and spelunking on the moon…just the sort of spiritual magicians she wanted to meet! But here was this reserved, wary monk. No fun at all! But he has potential, that is certain. Well, we'll see what we can do about that!, she mused and flashed him a peculiar smile, like that of the cat before it attacks the sparrow.

"Tell me," she said after a long silence, "why you are interested in the White Tiger Green Dragon? It is not so common among Taoists, and—let's face it!—after the initial novelty and excitement wear off, can be rather monotonous. At least as the Chinese practice it!"

There she was again! The insults and casual disregard for his feelings apparently were something he would have to get used to. She was, after all, his teacher, and he owed her the same respect he must show to a Taoist master at the White Crane. And who was to say but these barbs perhaps would have the same effect as a slap in the face in the Ch'an tradition!

"My master," he said with reserve, "is a master in the tantric arts and recommends them highly as a way to experience the way and its power, and to understand the underlying unity of material and nonmaterial worlds."

"Hmph!" said Lekshe. "Is that all? What about your experience in these matters. Come, you can tell me about them…yes, ALL about them! It is essential, you see, if I am to correct their errors. Or build," she said somewhat begrudgingly, "on their 'strengths.' But first, I was told you are a scholar as well as a neophyte tiger. Perhaps, as we get to know each other better, you can help me—I am only a poor princess, after all!—understand the eight stanzas of Ga-dam-ba Ge-shay Lang-ri-tang-ba, which have long intrigued and puzzled me, especially the one—it's the fourth, I believe—in which he states that he must learn to reverence evil beings as though they were the rarest of treasures! Now what could that mean? Do you think he was influenced by the Christian missionaries and their master's dharma on our responsibility to help all beings? Or his follower Paulus who taught that men must submit meekly to injustice and cruelty as though it were a divine gift? An odd philosophy, I should think! Fight back, I say, but also nourish one's essential nature quietly, joyfully, quietly within, hmm? So we are dualists, no? But dualists—fighters on the one hand, lovers on the other—whose opposites meet and mesh, and from whom some infinite unity emerges! Is this not so?"

Ming blushed and shrugged his shoulders with a slight smile. He did not know what to say! He had heard of none of these doctrines. Perhaps Master Wu had decided these thinkers were not worth bothering with or would impede him on the Way. Or possibly he had never heard of them either! How much knowledge was there on the other side of White Crane Mountain? What books must be housed in the Great Library at Llasa.

"What was your library like?" he asked, warming, and leaning forward. "I confess, I know little—nothing!—about the men and ideas of which you speak. Are they part of your tradition?"

Lekshe laughed hard, rolling on her back and kicking her feet in the air like a bear juggling a ball with all four paws. "No, they are far from my tradition," she said, leaning sideways and looking at him with flushed cheeks and sparkling eyes. "That is why I read them! That is why my uncle gave them—the books, the thoughts, the ideas—to me as the great gift (far rarer than Ga-dam-ba's suffering, I assure you!) before he fell out with the lamaist establishment and I wound up an exile in this dreary place. Oh, but the ideas, they can save you!" she lunged toward him dramatically. He did not jump this time, and they both laughed. "They take your mind and spirit into the colorful, bright world of the Illuminated One no matter where you may be confined, exiled, imprisoned."

"Yes," said Ming, becoming animated, "I know that this is so. But often, when the thoughts have tumbled through my brain at night, when my body was too weary to stop them, I have blamed my lack of skill in contemplation, my inability to stop..."

"...the chattering monkey mind!" she finished the sentence. "Yes, yes, they do tell us that, don't they. And it IS important to still the mind, to let the waters clear so the vision of the pure moon can shine undefiled. But the mind still needs to be nourished by ideas, just as the body must be fed by rice and vegetables and curdled milk...oh, sorry! I forgot how repulsive that it to Chinese!"

They laughed together at this, and he did not feel offended at all.

"Still," she continued, "how easy it is for our 'masters' to control us once they have trained us to still our questioning intelligence and to submit to their every whim."

Ming frowned. "I cannot believe that my Master Wu exploits his students or tries to control them purely for selfish reasons! Surely..."

"Can't you? Now listen," she rolled onto her stomach and rested her impertinent chin on clenched fists, "he may teach you many fine things, and may have convinced you it is for your own good. But haven't you pretty much surrendered to him everything that makes you what you are? You dress the way he tells you, you think his thoughts, you eat his food, you engage in ritual sex with his mistresses.."

"No! This is all too much!" Ming leapt to his feet. "I cannot have you attack or insinuate...his mistresses?" Ming softened and searched mentally for some clue or hint to dislodge this accusation which, frankly, had never occurred to him. "Well, not 'mistresses,'" he conceded. "Perhaps partners."

Lekshe grunted. "Of course, he has to test us out before allowing us to couple with his precious pupils!" Ming was aghast, but could say nothing. "Well, why not. It's not sex, is it. It's meditation. That makes it all right! Do you think he would give you a scholarship, paid by the funeral dues of half-starved farmers seeking monastic blessings, to screw the local women whenever you or he were so inclined? Of course not! No, call it meditation and it's all right."

"How can you say such a thing! The White Tiger Green Dragon is the highest form of self-knowledge, the path..."

"Stop it, right there!" she shouted, leaping up to him, and grabbing both his shoulders. "Don't tell me what you have been taught. Tell me what you know!"

The words rang in the silence that followed, echoing and reechoing within his ears, searing into the silence within him. His affronted gaze bore into Lekshe's glaring eyes; her unflinching vision burned deeply into his. At last his hands settled on her firm hips, and she pulled his body gently against her own.

"I want you to challenge what I say," she whispered. "To challenge what your master says. To come ALIVE!" her voice rose, then fell again into a caress, "to know from doing and being and becoming, not because you were told or inculcated or trained, like a parrot, to mouth other people's truths."

He closed his eyes and nodded. A powerful sense of physical attraction swept over him. He opened his eyes and looked with great tenderness and appreciation at the imposing woman before him. She slid her hands up the sides of his neck and cupped the sides of his face, drawing it to her like a great bowl of wine and drinking deeply from his open lips.

"It is all right," she said quietly, pulling him down onto the divan, "we won't be disturbed. I told the servant we would have an animated philosophical discussion and spend the rest of the day in meditation. He would never interrupt such a tedious assignation!"

*   *   *

Was he drugged? Or simply bewitched? Ming did not remember entering the intimate room, lined in old brocades the color of new hyacinths, where he now lay on a sweet-smelling bed. Lekshe sat beside him, her skin at once golden and rosy in the amber candlelight. He took her hand and breathed in the oily, musky scent, so unlike the fragrance of Chinese women. He closed his eyes, and felt the pleasing toughness of her fingers against his soft cheek.

"What kind of a beard is that!" she laughed, brushing his face briefly, and wedging herself between him and the wall. "No body at all! Like a boy's ponytail!" But she smiled in a way that showed she liked the fineness of his hair, and moved her free hand to the top of his head. For several minutes, she massaged his temples and stroked his face. Ming closed his eyes and yielded to the blissful sensations as her fingers fell like rain, or a gentle waterfall, over and over his cheekbones, up and down the bridge of his nose, onto his lips and back, beyond his ears.

Lekshe moved her face closer and closer to his left ear, humming softly as she massaged the nape of his neck and rubbed her fingers into the flesh beneath the earlobes. "I am in tune with the coming night," she murmured, half to herself. "With the rising moon, the waking of the owl." Her face brushed his and nuzzled his head, and one arm slid around his waist. "Do you feel the yang rising within you?"

He nodded wordlessly.

"Good!" she said abruptly, clasping him with surprising firmness against her hard body. She opened her mouth around the rim of his ear, and baring her teeth, bit quickly along the ridge, moving toward the ear canal with moist, firm motion. Her breath was warm and rhythmical and seemed to fill him with warmth.

"Ouch," he said sleepily. She laughed and pulled back, opening one of his eyes with her forefinger. "Hmm?" she asked softly, cocking her head. "You are not used to biting? Just wait!"

Lekshe drew back the clothing at his neck and opened the front with a dexterous movement of her hand. Her head slid under his beard, and she gently gnawed the flesh below his jaw, around his Adam's apple, sucking the skin in the hollow of his throat. He made a noise of unimaginable pleasure. She hummed back, and tenderly placed a claw-like hand on his chest, raking the hard nails just enough to leave a pink trail of sensation.

He squirmed a bit, and looked curiously into her eyes. "Don't worry!" she teased, "I don't have a knife! You will not suffer any flesh wounds, I promise you!"

"Are you certain this will lead…"

"…lead to what?" she asked saucily. "To sex? Of that I am certain! And such as you have never dreamt possible. But to enlightenment? That is up to you, my Ming. I provide the heat. You provide and nurture the fire. You must raise it up and nourish both of our chi through the intensity of your ardor. Now," she said, sinking back against the wall, "undress me. And do not be afraid to bite!"

*   *   *

Evening passed into nightfall, night into day. Days became weeks, and Ming lost track of time except to note whether the sun, the moon or stars greeted his view when he went out to exercise with Lekshe in the cold, open courtyard, and when they ate the unfamiliar Tibetan grains and meat soup in the adjacent lodge frequented by travelers from the West. At these times, Lekshe was as social as a madame, bubbling with enthusiasm as she talked with guests. Her ruddy cheeks had a special glow, he thought, observing quietly from the sidelines, foreign in language and appearance. Now and then, Lekshe would whisper with a small group, glance his way and they would laugh among themselves. She assured him later he had no reason to feel hurt and wounded. "I say nothing to them about our work!" she insisted, though there was always merriment in her voice, and some of it gently mocking. "They draw their own conclusions!"

At times, Ming would grasp her hands intently when she spoke to him about the guests and forget to eat, looking inquiringly into her eyes, as though he could find there the source of the Valley Spirit which was gradually opening up to him. At these times, she would not smile, but neither would she let him hold her gaze for long. "Work!" she would say, "do not think!"

"I cannot not think," he said to her one winter's night. She was wearing a vest of skins and heavy quilted trousers, having been outside. Her face was even more flushed than usual, her eyes teary from the cold.

"Very well, then," she said, her back to him. "What is it you think of."

"When we are locked in the dragon's embrace, I forget everything I have ever been taught. I must tell you something: that first day, when you fell out of the sky at me, I thought you were one of the wrathful dakinis I had heard of in my youth!"

Lekshe threw back her head and laughed heartily. "Yes, I can well imagine! Dakini: heavenly sky-tredders, the deity in its female principle. In legend, a blood-thirsty deva lusting for human meat! Tell me," she said, lowering her voice and drawing close, "what did your teachers tell you about these monsters!"

"Monsters, yes, but more…monsters and portals to Enlightenment, all in one!" he answered, as she knelt on her heels and listened. "Even I have read about the great Tibetan master, Naropa, and his encounter with one of these. The old witch rose up from the cemetery like a fume and surrounded him with her 37 hideous features."

"The blood-red eye!"

"The twisted nose!"

"Teeth turned inward into the foul smelling mouth and reeking of decay!" He made a face like a small boy tasting dung, and Lekshe roared until she fell backward, having to steady herself on one arm.

"I love it! It's great!" she cried. "The great hump-backed, wheezing, weeping, wrinkled virago with her flaming yellow beard!" She stopped suddenly, and bolted right up to Ming's face. "And so…what was the point!"

"The point," Ming repeated, his moment of fun unceremoniously deflated. "The point…."

"The hag asked Naropa the scholar what he knew about the dharma…the words, or the sense. He said the words, and she was dizzy with delight. But when he added 'as well as the sense,' she gnashed those decaying old teeth and beat her breast. Why was that?"

Ming did not reply. "It was only a story," he said, weakly, "told to terrify young boys into…"

Lekshe leapt to her feet and shook her head in both hands. "Your teachers are fools…or you are a fool for not listening to them entirely! The old woman is a projection of Naropa's own fears and inadequacies. She is the complement to his fine learning, yin to his yang. He is youthful, strong, brave but drowning in words, your own curse, Taoist. When he claims to have also the sense of the dharma, she collapses in grief because she knows he is lying, or innocently supposing he knows something far beyond his ken. Then, she takes him," Lekshe pounced and wrapped her arms around his neck, "and reveals to him the sublime truth beyond ugliness, beauty and mechanical knowledge!"

Ming whistled to himself. "That…is quite a twist! I think I have a better appreciation now of your paintings…."

"The blood red dakini is my favorite," said Lekshe, leaping before him in a provocative, but sinister pose, "with her girdle of bones and a blood-filled skull in her left hand!" She turned her back, chuckled and looked at him over her shoulder with a wink.

"So what words flow through you when we are together?" she asked. She unfastened her vest and let it slip onto the cushion along with her sword. Gingerly, like the dancer she was, she stepped out of the trousers and turned to him in her plain chemise.

"Initially, when we were first together, I would think through the instructions I had at the monastery, before I began the dual cultivation," Ming said. "I would recall the lessons of the masters and proceed with restraint."

She nodded, outwardly attentive but inwardly thinking to herself, "I cannot believe this boy. A boy's beard, a boy's simplicity. And yet he grows every day, and I grow with him!". "'There is nothing like restraint,'" she said, quoting Lao Tzu. "'Restraint begins with giving up one's own ideas. This depends on Virtue gathered in the past. If there is a good store of Virtue…'"

"'…then nothing is impossible.' Yes, that is part of it. Part of me obviously desires abandonment to the flesh…"

She lunged at him. He jumped, and leaned back into the couch.

"How can you speak like this? Twisted, prudish, perverted!" she yelled into his face, grabbing his shoulders, then pushing him back. He fell onto the couch, propped by his arm, one bare leg exposed as far as the hip. "I cannot believe it…you have practiced, what? Six months? And you still speak of 'desires,' 'flesh,' 'abandon,' like some Confucian censor!" She tore off her chemise, stood naked before him and placed a naked foot hard on his thigh. "This," she said, holding out both her breasts, "is Tara! Don't you feel the fire? This cultivation is the path. There is no other. There is no shame. Tu Ming," she said softly, easing herself onto his lap, "to abandon is exactly what you must do…and then to take that fire and lift it to the mysterious gate, where 'Your mouth cannot explain what appears before you; Seeing it would be relieved of all concern.'"

Ming caught his breath. "This is exactly true," he said, twisting his body toward hers. He rubbed his hand along the curve of her inner thigh and run it up, over her stomach, between her breasts and along the graceful line of her neck. He rested it on her cheek. "Drop down beside me," he said, and she did. He placed his wrist against her waist. His mind was agitated, as though two completely different streams of thought, segregated and separated until this moment, suddenly merged, thrashed and clawed at each other like two wild cats..like dragon and tiger..released in the same small space.

"I thought you Taoists were free," she said.

"If I survive this night," he said with some irony, sweat forming on his neck and trickling down his back, "I shall be." She smiled impishly and nodded. This is what he needed, she thought. It is all thrashing around inside him now. What energy will be unleashed! What power! I will ride this dragon to the very door of heaven. I will break it down and take him with me. "So tell me more," she said, "initially. What went through your mind."

"The teachings, the words." He squirmed out of his robe; the heat was intolerable. "Am I all right? Is it supposed to be like this?"

"Yes, yes! You've been stoking the furnace since the first sweet flags appeared in the woods."

"Could it be a fever?"

"A fever? Yes, but a fever of health, not illness. Keeping talking."

"Then, when the words receded, the sensations returned...the rhythm of Mei Cha , the undulations and contractions of Su Ba. the exquisite subtlety of Chou Yin."

"You relived each evolution, that is good," said Lekshe. She wiped his brow with an edge of sheeting. "But did you think about it?"

"Yes, yes in fact I did. But less and less, I admit, in recent weeks."

"They will recede into a pattern of pre-being," she said. "They will be lost to your consciousness, your mind, like the experiences of your mother's womb: important for who you become but a background for a new reality."

Lekshe put her arm around him and drew close. They were both damp with perspiration in the otherwise cool room. Lekshe half closed her eyelids and rolled her eyeballs up, feeling the golden aura rise between them, through them, out of them, like a halo in a thangka of two copulating deities. But as yet, there was no physical union between them.

"And what then?" she whispered, raking her nails softly along his spine.

"Then, the firing process," he said, his lips at her ear. "Grasping the ball of fire and lifting it up, up, up…."

At that moment, their cultivation began, unlike any previous that they had shared, unlike even like any Lekshe had experienced before. Their stomachs were two cauldrons groaning with heat, intensifying with each friction. The heat slowly rose through the sacral pump, into the warm region of the kidneys. Yang ascended, yin receded as Ming rose above her, in the position associated with healing, then fell upon her into the embrace of nine pulses, then under her in the posture which quickens the blood, and finally, as the heat left the cauldron in a spasm which convulsed both of their bodies, into one unity through which the flame rose higher and higher, dangerously into the region of the heart. There it divided in two and continued throughout the night, riding on the lightness of breath, in and out, out and in.

At last, Lekshe's mouth covered his own and, as she massaged the base of his spine, she gently gnawed at his lips and pulled the fire to a greater height by the suction of her breath, aware of the danger of losing it through the orifice. He twitched, she blew, the kiss intensified beyond the limitations of flesh, and the fire, as she directed it with her lips and very breathing, roared into the center of bliss. Ming gasped, Lekshe clutched him more tightly, and together, they rode on the peak of the flame and soared into the Golden Field.

*   *   *

"It is a letter. From your Master Wu." Lekshe was not her usual cheerful self. Ming had been preparing correspondence for a local beer merchant. Like Wu, Lekshe had reassured him that honest work complemented the serious cultivation of the internal alchemy, quoting Man-An, "There is nothing better than concentration in activity." And again, "You need not necessarily prefer stillness," (An Elementary Talk on Zen," Minding Mind, trs. T. Cleary, 1995, Shambhala) though stillness had certainly played a minor role in their energetic practice.

Ming looked up. It was by now a familiar message, one he had expected for some time. Lekshe knelt down beside him and placed the unsealed letter on top of the desk. He put down his brush and looked sadly into her eyes. She softly placed a hand on his arm and returned a gaze of deep concern and empathy.

"Well, open it!" said Lekshe at last, tapping the missive impatiently. "I am certain it is time for you to go on to the next level of White Dragon! You must leave."

Ming shook his head and placed his hand over hers.

"I shall not."

Lekshe felt a warm glow rise from her heart, started to smile with delight, then stopped abruptly.

"Do not be stupid!" she answered, pulling away her hand. "We have both advanced to the gate, but can go no further. There has been no advancement in the past two months, surely you have seen that." She rubbed the top of his head. "The Mysterious Pass...here!" she pressed a soft spot on his crown, "has not opened for you..." She referred to the initiate's practice which results in an actual hole opening on the back of the skull as an enlightened state develops and matures. The Vajrayana (Tibetan Buddhism) believes this is also where the spirit exits in death.

"That is a Tibetan custom," he rejoined, "it has nothing to do with the Tao."

"Who is the teacher here anyway!" she countered, springing to her feet. "Did not Wu send you here to learn the Tibetan path of the tantric arts?"

She pulled his robe down over his shoulder, where neat rows of bruises and small scars from bites and scratches appeared as evidence of his cultivation. "But the most important evidence, the opening of the Mysterious Pass on the crown of the head, it has not occurred. Perhaps," she shrugged, "it is a purely Buddhist practice. We have been too eclectic."

"Do not say that," he countered, rising. "If you have taught me one thing, Lekshe Tsogyel, it is the gospel of unity: unity of the White Tiger, Green Dragon, the unity of our different traditions, the singularity of understanding and unspeakable bliss. I do not feel we are very short of the goal…"

"But we are," she swirled to face him, hardening her features, toughening her racing heart. "We have taken the fire to the Golden Field where it will rage out of control."

"We will channel it."

"We have no power to do so. You must return to the White Crane. This is a critical stage for you. You must create within yourself a new spiritual body out of this immortal Foetus."

"I am sick of alchemy!" he shouted, slamming the desk against the wall. The ink pot flooded the beer merchant's letter and began to saturate Wu's scroll when Lekshe plucked it from the black pool and wiped it on the sleeve of her dark tunic.

"And I am sick of you!" she yelled back, lying from the bottom of her heart. She broke the seal, and read. "Yes, it is a summons. You have two weeks to prepare. He wonders why you have not communicated with him, whether you are well. Ming, you really must reply to him," she said, her voice softening. "It was he who has directed your practice to date. It is he who will lift you up to the highest."

Ming wiped the sweat from his brow. "It is you who have lifted me up. You are my teacher. We are one."

"We are two," she said coldly, "and only in our practice, for a few hours, do we transcend that dualism and ride the dragon as a single spirit. You must go."

Ming was silent. He dropped to the floor in the lotus position, not to meditate, but to gather his thoughts. After some time, he said:

"All right. I will leave. I thank you for all you have done for me. You are the greatest teacher I have ever known. I will leave, but not for Wu, not for the life I once had. Within Taoism, there is a tradition of wanderers, you know that yourself."

"Don't be ridiculous...how will you support yourself, how will you find the self-discipline to continue your practice? This is madness!"

"I have my work as a scribe. I cannot continue this life of bouncing back and forth, up and down, scaling the heights, crashing down to the ordinary. I will continue my practice, alone if necessary. I have learned so much, from all of my partners, but especially from you. These lessons cannot be forgotten. Rather than return to the unbearable routine of the monastery, so empty of love, I will set out in the world and seek other teachers, other paths. I know I can only go forward, not back."

Lekshe looked at him longingly. She valued her own practice as highly as his. It was true, she had broken through a longstanding block during the past several months with him. She knew full well the name of her new obstacle to growth. It was her love of Ming. Let him go, her mind said. Let him follow his own path. For though the goal is the same, you must take a different route. You are two, not one.

"My uncle knows many merchants who would be pleased by your workmanship," she said. "Let me have him provide you with letters of introduction." Ming nodded his gratitude. "You will need some money to get started on your way. No, do not protest, it does me no good. I have more than enough, surely you've seen that." She walked to a chest by the door and produced a pouch of coins. "Hide it well, though monks are seldom waylaid by bandits in these parts."

Ming accepted the offering and held Lekshe's hand warmly. Looking into her eyes again, he thought, "I have come perilously close to falling in love. I am grateful she does not love me, except as a student."

Looking into his eyes, Lekshe thought, "He has never loved me. But we have had an exceptional cultivation. How will I ever find another partner so tender and willing to learn?"

He drew her close, kissed her lightly once and decided not to question the rapid beating of her heart.

                    *   *   *

Wu raised an eyebrow as the servant presented the letter from Tu Ming. He did not expect a written reply, but rather suspected the young man would appear at his door as summoned on this particular day in late winter. If something were wrong, the letter would not be from Ming. Yet, something was wrong, since it was mere paper, not Ming, that was before him now. He dismissed the servant, and looked over at Shan, who was beside him in the sun room tending to the hearty plants which thrived there in the colder months.

"Read this for me, will you?" he asked.

Shan put down his shears and took the letter.

"'Estimable Master,'" he read, "'Please accept my deepest apologies for not writing sooner. As you may well imagine, my cultivation has been proceeding at an extraordinary pace. Lekshe Tsogyel is the finest teacher I have yet encountered (not including your own eminence, of course). "

Wu sighed. "Go on, go on, though I know what's coming next!"

"'I have reached a breakthrough in my practice which has revealed to me the most sublime power of the Tao and it's real seat within the mind.'" Wu grunted, though Shan was not sure whether it was from satisfaction or exasperation. "'Because of this...'"

"I will not be returning to the White Crane...now or at any time in the foreseeable future." said Wu.

"But how did you know?" asked Shan, used to being amazed by his friend's prescience.

"And what are the exact words?"

"'I have decided to leave the order and pursue a life as a wandering Taoist monk, making my living as a scribe, and seeking to build upon the cultivation in which I have advanced so markedly.'"

"Wu, this is a great loss for us!" Shan interjected. "Tu Ming is widely regarded as your logical successor.

After a pause, Wu reared his head back and roared with laughter.

He laughed until his cheeks were red, and tears rolled down his face. Shan smiled sheepishly and let the attack run its course. He had only seen Wu laugh out loud once before, when a report arrived indicating that a particularly annoying Confucian censor had fallen from his horse near the Yuan T'ai brook and lost an entire portfolio of evidence alleging immorality at a neighboring temple.

"He…he is almost there!" said Wu, between gasps for air, brushing the tears from his cheeks. Shan slapped Wu on the shoulders and shook him with delight. "This is great news, Wu! Is this what you were expecting?

Wu blew his nose into his handkerchief, and rubbed his eyes one more time. "No," he said, "but it is what I had been hoping for!"

*   *   *

"Very well!" announced Lekshe the evening before Ming's departure. "We must have one final ride before you leave. You must have a good store of essence to start your adventure, since it may be some time," she winked, "before you encounter a female adept of my abilities!"

Ming laughed, and finished off his evening rice. "You have certainly changed my thinking about the dual cultivation," he said, warmly.

"What do you mean? " she asked. "Did you think that women were vessels only, here for your use, with no capacity to ride the wind and roll with the white clouds themselves?"

"In fact, yes, though I knew that Wu had the highest opinion of his own partners, especially the one of recent years."

"Man, woman, beggar, king…what difference does it make?" asked Lekshe. "You draw in my female energy, I absorb your yang. I give, you take. You take, I give. It is a cycle, is it not, like any other? " She drew him into the adjoining chamber where they had spent a hundred nights in ecstatic cultivation. "You have felt my fire against your fire." He pulled her close, his hand between their bellies. "The myth that man feeds on and depletes the female essence is a superstition that has endured for thousands of years. There is no basis to it! The alchemy is dual, not singular. I am not wood to your fire. We, together, are wood and air, essential for fire to live."

"I feel free," he said, allowing himself to be drawn onto the divan for the last time.

"It will not last," she said, dotting his lips with small hot kisses and ringing his ears with soft bites. "You will grow hungry, cold. You may give up the path altogether!"

"Impossible!" he countered, easing her under his body and unloosening her silk sash. "Once you have seen the sun, how can you settle for a life of darkness? You have shown me the source of radiance and warmth and nourishment."

"For me, you have opened the doors to the actual experience of states I had only encountered in books and scriptures," she said intently, thinking, "I will long for you forever, and this longing will serve to carry me high into the white clouds, into the nirvana I now know is real."

CHAPTER VII

▼

NI HUAN, THE BRAIN

Tu Ming brushed the snow off his shoulders and looked up at the sign over the inn on the edge of Hsun-yang. Despite the weather, the street brimmed with busy townspeople coming and going with the day's work. Ming had been alone for a week now, since bidding farewell to Dran-son, who went back to the Tibetan-Chinese community where his language and cultural skills were in high demand. The city of Hsun-yang reminded Ming of Hsienyang where he had visited The Yellow Bud. He turned and looked back at the bridge he had just crossed, now a ghostly frame half lost in the haze. The trot of rickshaws echoed among the bare trees and austere buildings, rhythmic, almost as though keeping time with the silent downward spiral of the falling snow. Ming rested his hand over the pouch of coins under his robe. Hungry and thirsty for tea, he was beginning to understand the forces which motivated men who had never tasted the highest bliss and led them away from the pure contemplation of the Tao to a life dedicated to palliating ever-new desires. Hsun-yang had something of a reputation as a center for the arts and sciences. There were several highly regarded schools, monastic centers of all philosophies and even a Western missionary outpost. An active business community promised to offer employment to a learned scribe with a talent for languages. He shook the snow from his feet and entered a surprisingly bright hostel, with large windows which let in the strong white light.

It was late for mid-day rice and early for the evening trade, but the inn was as busy as the streets outside as travelers, traders and servants stole a few moments of warmth and refreshment in the midst of the day. Ming chose an inconspicuous corner away from the glare and gratefully sipped the dark tea brought quickly by a waiter obviously keen to earn merit through prompt service. Blowing on his fingers to warm them, Ming sat back and closed his eyes, oblivious to those around him. He was soon asleep.

He slipped lightly from the world of red dust into the land of dreams, an exotic garden filled with peonies, plum blossoms and jasmine, all growing profusely together despite their different seasons. A goldfish pool lay in the center. He looked into the pool, as still as glass, and saw, not his own image, but a raptor with fierce, hooked beak and erect plumage. The bird rose from the pool with a mighty splash, a phoenix with a wing span the length of three men. He flapped his wings and soared over the fragrant garden toward the sun. As he disappeared from view, an eclipse stole the sun and Ming feared the raptor had devoured it. But it turned gradually into the moon, full and bright, and moonlit nighttime fell upon the scene. Luscious white lotus buds popped up on the surface of the water and opened into blossoms as wide as a maiden's arm. One blossom in the center shot up on a slender stalk, pointing to the moon. As Ming looked up, a bright light began to glow on the moonscape, growing larger and larger, moving toward the earth. As it approached, Ming saw a woman— undoubtedly the moon goddess herself—descending through the heavens on the back of a writhing jade green dragon. She was enrobed in sheer white clouds; her hair was like tendrils of living silver, her fingernails, small talons, emitted sparks like many colored jewels as she floated closer to Ming. He felt queasy, a bit sea sick and looked below to find he was on the back of a large white tiger, the deep ostinato growl rocking him gently back and forth. The dragon landed in the pool with a great roar, a flurry of spray and battening wings, wrapping its tail around the lotus stalk like a caduceus, breathing waves of silver fire into the now frosty night air. The white lotuses shrunk to the edge of the pool, ringing the beast and his beautiful consort.

The tiger reared back and thrust into the pool, filling Ming with terror. He dug his fingers deep into the stiff white fur, but fell backward into water which was not wet, but the texture of fine quilted silk. It undulated sensuously beneath him, rolling his body away from the center. The goddess slid from the back of the dragon and walked steadily across the silken sea, covering him with her cloudy raiment. She opened her dark red lips over his mouth and dissolved her body into his. Like clouds, they melted together. The dragon and tiger, now intertwined, were suddenly beneath them. There was no sound but a deep sigh of contentment and a rush of heat, like a fountainhead, springing from their midst in the cool air. Soon there were not four forms, but one: invisible but deeply felt. He felt himself sinking deeper, deeper into the pool, the silk weighing heavy on his face, heavier than the goddess' siphoning kiss.

He awoke, gasping for air, flushed and confused. An older couple chuckled, looking his way. "Shellfish!" the old man clucked, wagging his finger. Ming smiled weakly back, and took a deep breath. Other sounds seeped into his emerging consciousness. The clatter of tea utensils, the cook coughing, the rattle of the ancient beams under a sudden shower.

"Five or seven characters to a line…what difference does it make! Do you think the Eight Immortals give a chicken's gizzard whether there are five or forty…."

"Forty! You are ridiculous, Shen T'ao! How could you replicate the exact pattern of the four tones in couplets with so many characters."

"I agree with Wan Su. There is symmetry and tradition in these forms. They are ordained by the gods!"

Ming rubbed his eyes with his sleeve and looked down at his cold tea. He listened to the voices—two male, one female—behind the screen to his left.

"Another Confucian ruse to control the masses. Now, the people—well, sometimes I can see the need for a little political discipline. But in rhymed literature? Never!"

"Hush! You never know who is at the next table. Do you want to spend any more time in confinement."

"Worse yet," whispered the other male voice, "drag us innocent bystanders into it!" They all laughed. Ming heard the gurgle of tea being poured.

"But Liu Chang-ch'ing had no problem with the perfect rhyme, the Imperially sanctioned prescription for writing verse."

"Wen Kuang, of course he didn't!" the woman's voice interjected. "He lived a thousand years ago! Must we continue to follow the footsteps of our aesthetic ancestors into perpetuity? These are modern times! The world is changing. Our verse must reflect what we have become, what we aspire to, not the antiquated rumblings of the dead!"

Ming stretched but lost his balance, tumbling against the screen.

"Excuse me, please, venerable sirs…and…and…"

As he scrambled to his feet to grimaces of annoyance from the two men, he was taken aback by the bemused, merry eyes of the contentious woman whose voice had drawn him out of his bizarre fantasy.

"Watch yourself! Spying on our conversation, were you monk?" retorted one of the men.

"Perhaps this Taoist is in league with the Confucians, and interested in making a little money on the side!" quipped the other dryly.

"On the contrary," offered the woman Shen T'ao, drawing up her legs sideways on the bench. "He may well be a Taoist poet in the great tradition you've just defended, Wen. So what do you have to say for yourself, monk? A little eavesdropping to improve your trade?"

Ming was flustered and bowed many times, pumping his hands for forgiveness. "I give you my word, honorables," he said, head bowed, "that I was not intentionally listening to your conversation. It's just," he looked up weakly, "that it awoke me from sleep and…"

"Sleep!" All three laughed heartily, giving each other knowing glances.

"Then everything we've heard about Taoist monks is true?" said Wan Su, a tall, burly, heavily bearded man in antique clothing. "Lazy good-for nothings!"

"Living off the superstitions of simple countryfolk…." Wen added.

"Hocus pocus!" laughed Shen T'ao. "Now there's a rhyme for you!" she said, nodding to Wan.

"Hocus pocus…stroke us!" replied Wan, leaning over to Shen, narrowing his eyes and winking suggestively. The three burst into another gale of laughter. Ming was fully awake now, and beginning to feel less an oafish victim of their sophistication and more of a partner, a fourth element enlivening their conversation.

"Yes," said Wen, "perhaps this monk is adept in the famous 'dual cultivation.' The subject of much literature…"

"…so I've heard…." Wan added.

"…so my mother told me," winked Shen.

"And speaking of duels," said Wan, "perhaps this monk would care join us in some verbal repostes and drink some of our fine tea to refresh his obviously careworn brain!"

"Careworn?" queried Wen, screwing up his face as to a puzzle. "More likely calcified by priests' talk and staying up too late staring blankly at a bare wall…."

"And eating stew made from raw bean curd and willow shoots," added Shen. "And drinking barley water…"

"…and only reading about wine in Tu Fu!"

"So, you propose to whine about tofu?" asked Ming whimsically, swinging his leg over the bench next to Wen and sitting down like a old friend. Wen, a short, thin scholar with laugh lines around his eyes, raised an eyebrow comically and leaned back as though being visited by a leper. The others chuckled, then Wen bounced back and gave Ming a good-natured slap on the back.

"So, introduce yourself, monk," said Shen T'ao, pushing back her black braid, "before you make any more terrible puns!" She clapped for another tea cup, as Ming settled himself among them.

"I am Tu Ming, a Taoist monk formerly of the White Crane Hermitage," he said simply, looking somewhat quizzically at Shen T'ao.

"Shen T'ao," Wan whispered obviously into her ear so all could hear, "I think he is trying to figure out who you are!"

"A mysterious concubine from the Imperial court?" she replied in a stylized high-pitched voice that made Wen plug his fingers in his ears.

"A strumpet escaped from the Ch'ing Lan Brothers' Traveling Magic Show?" gasped Wen.

"Mother Kuan Yin herself, taking a break from performing acts of mercy!" said Wan. "Now, isn't it perfectly obvious!"

"Actually," said Ming, "I think I have fallen into the clutches of a band of….poets! Am I right?

"Poets! What? You accuse your hosts of being godless renegades?"

"Conjurers of bad rhymes and worse tonal patterns?"

"Swillers of vile beer and eaters of pork snout pies?" asked Shen T'ao in mock horror. "Yes!" she said, dropping all pretense and smiling honestly. "We are poets, of one sort or another. But is this a profession you know something about?"

"A profession, no," conceded Ming. "A practice, perhaps."

"You are a poet yourself!" exclaimed Wen. Then, narrowing his eyes, mischievously, "…not unlike the great T'ang Taoists, I would presume."

"Oh, no," Ming said, with a slight laugh, "nothing so excellent, not by far. I have not the patience, discipline or talent to express my wonder at the beauties of nature in the elegant poetic designs perfected more than a thousand summers past."

"Well, let's hear one of your poems, monk," said Wan. "It's all right...we won't roast you to a crisp if your rhymes are trite or your rhythms rock like a flower boat in a storm!"

"You are just a monk, to your credit!" added Wen.

"And surely we'd lose merit in the next life if we mocked your modest efforts!" said Shen T'ao.

Ming noticed the lute beside Shen T'ao and indicated with a movement of eyebrows and fingers that he would like to test it. Shen T'ao narrowed her eyes approvingly, and passed the old instrument along to him.

Ming propped it on his thigh and strummed several times. "Ah," he murmured, "this is elegant. Very old, very true," he said, looking up, into Shen T'ao's eyes.

"Yes, it belonged to my family for my generations. "

He inhaled the fragrance of oils and resins which had been lovingly massaged into its thin, resilient wood. Shen T'ao watched him closely. To appreciate the instrument so keenly before playing is truly rare, she thought. He is either a great musician or great poet. Or something else.

Ming was neither a great musician or poet, but, as Shen T'ao intuited, was capable of great, consuming love, a love which had no object except love itself. His unpracticed fingers trembled slightly as he caressed a simple accompaniment out of the stained, ancient wood. Its hollow resonated beneath the quivering strings.

Too long have I wandered from Kuan Kei Mountain,
My childhood home. Often, on nights like this,
When the moon floods the city with enchanting light,
I hear my mother's voice, calling for me deep among the woods,
Sweeter than any thrush's song, more soothing than the owl.
A warm breeze penetrates the cold night air. I turn.
But not even her ghost is there to comfort me.
The empty tea bowl in my hand is fuller
Than my heart.

"Bravo, monk!" exclaimed Wen, patting him on the back. "What do you think, friends?"

Wen and Wan exchanged animated words of encouragement and began to chatter about the similarities to Po Chuan and other T'ang masters, though Ming thought their sentiments were rather exaggerated. His dark eyes, mild and full, rose to meet Shen T'ao's.

"I too lost my mother when I was young," she said quietly, touching his hand. "Here…" She reached for the lute which he surrendered.

Shen T'ao slid her hand several times up and down the lute's slim neck, grasping it at last at the base where it joins the body. She looked to the side as she played, sure and well practiced, while she spoke as though to herself.

Gone the moth eyebrows, rouge, the natural blush of my cheek.
My robe is drab; white tresses curl about my jade hair ornament.
Why maintain pretense, now that my husband is gone this winter
Into the land of the blue cliffs? I have wealth, esteem among my peers.
And yet, looking in my mirror this morning, there is no one there
But the specter of my mother's memory.

Ming's breathing nearly stopped. Wan and Wen had slipped away, extending their discussion to the decadence of Li Ho, but neither Ming nor Shen T'ao noticed. Shen T'ao looked up at him, directly, a clear, honest and open expression on her face. Ming looked questioning at her, but there was no particular question in his mind.

"I see you know what it is like to be alone," he said.

She laughed a little. "I am not alone, " she said. "Surely, as a student of the Tao, you know we have but one Mother."

"Mother, yes, Mother capital 'M'!" he said. "But the haunting sense of loss…"

"The melancholy…."

"The hunger for something, someone no longer there…."

"…is not easy to forget. It is a wound which time does not heal."

Ming sat back and withdrew into himself.

"You are with her now, aren't you?" said Shen T'ao watching. "Her with a capital 'H'!"

"Yes," he said, with closed eyes, then, opening them, "you are clearly a scholar, quite unusual for a woman."

"There are many unusual women in these parts," she said, with a sly smile. He nodded. That certainly had been his experience in the past year!

"My father left everything to me," she continued, sitting back, cross-legged. "As his only child with his favorite wife, I was, I suppose, indulged. Indulged in books and poetry and music. And educated by an old Taoist tutor, so I knew the Tao Te Ching before I could recite the Analects!"

"That is extraordinary!" he responded, jolted out of his reverie. "And your father...he didn't think this education was...."

"Wasted on a girl? Oh, I am certain he was disappointed that he did not have a son by Chu Sung! But he was quite an unconventional thinker, perhaps because he peppered his bland Confucianism with the salt of Taoist irreverence!"

"So what do you do? Talking and drinking tea in public with men..."

"Like a common pillow girl? My poetry earns me the right to associate with men of lesser talent!" she said wryly. "Provided I do not antagonize the other women in the community, or give them ideas! No, it is not what it seems. I am tolerated as a novelty, a freak of nature, a man in a woman's body, as Wan has called me. Though naturally, as now, when they must heed a call of nature, I am left to my own designs...and thank goodness!"

They both laughed. "And what of you, Venerable Tu Ming...."

"Ming, if you please. I am now disassociated with my hermitage."

She wrinkled her brow. "Was there trouble of some sort?" She liked the monk, who seemed a few years her junior and not as sophisticated as he should be. She continued to strum lightly, distractedly on the lute, pausing periodically to tune its white jade pegs.

"No trouble. It was the direction of my cultivation. It...wasn't pro-ceeding as productively as it might. I thought, perhaps...I would follow the Taoist practice of independent wandering for a while, to see if it…would improve." He stammered, looking for appropriate words.

"Hm! " exclaimed Shen T'ao, folding her arms across her chest. "I know how tedious those disciplines can be! My tutor—who was a woman by the way!—spent many years teaching me to stand like a crane, stoop like a duck and slither like a snake in pursuit of the inscrutable Tao…with little luck! Though I can do wonderful barnyard impersonations!"

Ming laughed. "Yes, I've tried a few of those, and more!"

"Tell me," she said, looking down at the lute, "have you ever explored some of the more…esoteric practices of Taoism."

Ming paused. "There are few that are not taught to the monks of the White Crane," he said, choosing his words carefully.

Shen T'ao nodded. "Yes," she said, "my tutor also initiated me into some of the higher planes of Taoist practice. She was a very energetic, seasoned…shall I say, supple teacher." Shen T'ao also seemed reluctant to say any more. "Fortunately," she said, with a sigh of relief, not knowing how to continue the conversation in this vein, "I have found in poetry an appropriate outlet for the passion which many direct toward pursuit of the Tao."

Ming looked even more closely at Shen T'ao. She was clearly the most remarkable woman he had ever met. There was an air of nobility and poise about her, an aura of wisdom as well as knowledge, and then there was her occupation. A poet! Not a prostitute, concubine or wife or mother, though she might be one or more of those. Not a farmer, herb gatherer or fisher. But someone who was educated in subtleties of rhyme, tone and narrative and whose work was read and debated by scholars, probably even outside of the region, possibly throughout the Empire.

Ming needed to make arrangements for his living quarters and to find the merchant for whom Lekshe Tsogyal had provided a letter of introduction. "Please feel free to talk to me again," he said, bowing. "I will be in this area for some time if my appointment is productive. "

"You will sometimes find me here with my friends, or at the Three Lilies House on the edge of town," she said, as no other woman would dare to say, not even to a celibate monk. "Please join our poetry readings. Perhaps we can also discuss your cultivation, for I have some special expertise in this area," she added.

The past year had resulted in the development of a great sensitivity in Ming toward women. In fact, he no longer craved the company of men, which in part accounted for his desire not to return to the monotony of the White Crane. It was more than sex. It was the Mother of all things which seemed to attract him to the female principle as never before. But when he left Shen T'ao and went in search of lodging, he felt a sense of weakness and separation. It was as though the tea cup were empty once again.

*   *   *

Wu was very busy in his office, Master Shan observed with no small curiosity. In addition to the usual administrative petitions and requisitions, Wu was engaged throughout the morning in the composition of five letters (Shan had made careful note of the number) which he wrote out himself in his eccentric, though decorative calligraphy. Throughout the process, Wu would variously chuckle to himself, gaze into the distance (often through Shan as though he were transparent), toss back his head in mirth, clap for a serving boy, then forget why he summoned him. Several hours and many erratic moods later, he was done, and, noting Shan lingering nearby, waved him closer.

"Shan! Here—see that these are sent immediately!" he said, beaming in an uncharacteristic display of elevated emotion. Shan looked at him thoughtfully, deciding he looked more like an aging athlete who had just run a race, or a horseman after a brisk, satisfying jaunt through the hills. Wu dropped the missives in Shan's sleeve and turned introspectively, humming and occasionally chuckling to himself. The vagaries of age, Shan thought to himself, as he left; but was that it? He pulled out the letters directly and read the addresses, only two of which were familiar to him. Beneath the address, each parcel bore the symbol of an I Ching hexagram. The first parcel was:

25 Fidelity

The next four, grouped together, were:

22 Adornment

45 Gathering

31 Sensitivity

30 Fire

The final one was:

2 Earth

He paused and stroked his beard thoughtfully, looked to see who was near…then changed his mind. Wu was his friend as well as master. If the secrets contained in these letters were any concern of his, truly he would soon know. He pocketed the documents again, and strode off to the stable.

*   *   *

Shang Po smiled quietly to herself as she opened the parcel brought by her girl. "It is from the hermitage!" the child exclaimed, with wide eyes. "A horseman brought it today!"

Shang Po looked at the distinctive calligraphy and the figure for "Fidelity" below. She dismissed the girl and took the parcel outside into the garden, where she had just been planting squash seedlings. She brushed the earth from her fingers onto her apron and opened the letter with a deep sense of satisfaction.

"The time has come for both of us," she read, as Wu had taught her, holding the parchment at arm's length to see better. "For Ming and myself," it continued. She read the line again, in a blur. Her brow furrowed, she placed the letter down. This was not what she had expected. She sat a while, looking absently out toward the hills, where her old partner lived. She picked up the page and read further. "Two destinies, separated by time. His?

You must write…" Here he gave instructions for her to send a message to Hsun-yang directly.

"Mine?" he continued. "Let me say this: my reading is 'Return.' I cannot tell you how I look forward to coming back to you before the dragonflies are on Wei River again, to stay with you forever in eternal youth." Shang Po gave a cry of joy and crushed the paper in both hands, but quickly caught herself and smoothed it out on her lap. She would go into town the next morning and find a scribe to put the necessary words to paper and send them off to the city Hsun-yang. Two destinies, yes, but only one of any real importance to her: an end to separation, forever.

*   *   *

The next four letters were received over the course of two weeks and were either read or listened to, depending on the level of literacy of the individual. Nothing very complex was asked of them, and the process was pleasant, though touched by wistfulness for several. Some distance away, Wu imagined with glee their receipt of his letters and laughed as each day's nurturing sun arose, bring him closer to his goal. If only all would go according to plan! But what was his plan, after all, compared with the great, seemingly random order of the Tao. Mysterious! Difficult to approach! And yet very definitely attainable.

"How could I have missed it?" he asked Shan over and over again. "Missed what?" his friend asked, until it became a ridiculous reply and he said nothing at all.

*   *   *

Shen T'ao put her pen aside to inhale the hyacinths her servant, Ma Lung, placed at her elbow. "Oh, these are wonderful!" sighed Shen T'ao, looking up at her good friend, whom she had bought to save from exile five years before. Ma Lung put her hand on Shen T'ao's shoulder and drew near. "As sweet as mistress," she whispered into her ear. Shen T'ao laughed, but to Ma Lung it was not the full, rich laugh she had known in happier times. "What is it that disturbs you,?" she said, stroking T'ao's thick, lustrous hair.

Shen took another deep breath of perfume from the white blossoms and took Ma Lung's small hand in hers. "For once, I do not know what to do," she said. "No, I doubt you can help me. I have met an unusual man—a monk, but no longer cloistered."

"A poet?" asked Ma Lung, sitting down beside her.

"A poet, a thinker, and, I believe, a practitioner of our art."

Ma Lung looked surprised. "In this area, it is quite rare. And dangerous!"

Shen T'ao nodded. "Yes, it is ironic, that the highest art can be practiced freely by women, whom the authorities consider only worthy to be wives, concubines and prostitutes, but men, especially the religious orders, are immediately suspect of degeneracy if they engage in the practice!"

Ma Lung laughed. She was small, elfin creature, with a sense of mischief and play which counterpointed nicely against her friend's more serious presence and droll irony. "Well, did he seem degenerate to you?"

Shen T'ao did not reply. She patted Ma Lung's hand and indicated she wished to return to her writing. "There will be some fierce competition at tomorrow's banquet," she noted, "I'd better sharpen my wits against that lot!"

Ma Lung was about to leave, when she turned suddenly. "Oh, excuse me, I have forgotten these!" She pulled two letters out of her sleeve and handed them to Shen T'ao. Shen put down her brush and looked at them with great curiosity. "Earth!" she read, then looking up at Lung, "What could this mean? Stay with me a moment…"

Lung sat down beside her as as T'ao unwound both scrolls and placed them side by side on her writing board.

"This is most extraordinary!" exclaimed Lung, looking over T'ao's shoulder. "This Tu Ming…would he be the monk you have been talking about? And who are these correspondents…'Adornment!' And 'Sensitivity!' They sound like characters in an opera…"

"Or definitive character types from the I Ching," mused T'ao. "Yes, this is most extraordinary. Apparently, they have both, at different times, compounded the cinnabar elixir with Tu Ming, and rode with him on the back of the white tiger into the heart of eternal fire. And they suggest I am the one to bring both him and myself to the ultimate ecstasy!"

Ma Lung laughed again. "Could this be a trick? Do you have any poetic enemies who would stop at nothing to put you in the hands of the Confucian authorities?"

"It's not without possibility," said T'ao thoughtfully. "And yet...." She was about to read the letters again, when a messenger came to the room.

"Three parcels, missy. Thank you!" he accepted a coin from Ma Lung and departed quickly.

Shen T'ao and Ma Lung exchanged glances. "'Gathering,'" said Ma Lung.

"'Fire,'" said Shen T'ao. "And this one: 'Fidelity.'" She unwrapped the scrolls in her hand and both women read greedily three additional tales of amazing detail and candid disclosure.

"It is no joke," said Ma Lung, at last, wiping a light sweat from her forehead. "Shall I go find him? This isn't something you want to lose!"

"Wait," said Shen T'ao, touching her friend's arm. "Let him come to me. My whereabouts is not very difficult to determine. Today, or perhaps tomorrow at the banquet, I will tell him of my knowledge of the White Tiger, Green Dragon. Then we will see what develops!"

*   *   *

Though satisfied with his appointment to a cloth merchant, and otherwise busy with cultivation, calligraphy and a bit of spring nature poetry, Tu Ming missed the society of his peers, and was delighted to receive Wen Kuang's invitation to the Peach Blossom Festival banquet at the home of his uncle, a minor official and patron of the arts. After his late winter's wanderings, he thought he had never experienced such a spring and craved the kind of celebration the banquet promised. "You'll find your 'new old friends' here in full force," promised Wan's words. Ming hoped that the poet Shen T'ao was among them. The scent of the lilies at his window, the rays of the warming sun, the cheerful morning chatter of a choir of birds all were almost too much to bear, awakening a kind of eroticism which filled every pore of his being. He carefully directed his passionate energy into his practice, heating the lower burner and now regularly experiencing the heat as it rose through the central column within, until his ch'i circulated freely and warmly throughout his body and saturated his mind in its hot golden light. His body took on a new sense of poise and beauty; his skin glowed, his eyes shone clear, as though bathed in an immortal spring. His employer had fitted him with a handsome, fresh suit of clothing, and he was able to buy new slippers with part of his earnings. In this mood, a blend of vigor, new energy and erotic intoxication, did Ming enter the banquet house and cause more than a few guests to top in mid-conversation and look with admiration and wonder in his direction.

Among them was Shen T'ao, in a peach robe appropriate to the occasion, her hair intertwined with pale, delicately scented blossoms, her skin even fairer except for a rush of color in her cheeks. Her stylized makeup was elegantly done, with long streaks of lavender and jade green brushed out beyond her eyebrows. The buzz of voices continued, but to these two, separated by an entire table and a throng of guests, the counterpoint of conversations was a blur; each stood isolated in a point in time defined by awareness of the other.

"Ah, our good monk friend, Tu Ming! I am so delighted you are able to honor us with your presence. This place is most unworthy to accept so learned and talented a guest!" effused Wen Kuang, surrounding Ming with his sleeves and good wishes, just as the monk had spied Shen T'ao across the room. "But we are ready to dine and drink, and then! the best part of all! You get to hear me recite my latest poem!" He laughed raucously, as he shepherded Tu Ming to a cushion at the far end of the table. Ming thanked him, wishing he could sit closer to Shen T'ao, at least to speak to her briefly, but he was pleased that at least he had a good view of her from this vantage point. In fact, she looked his way and nodded, with a lovely smile. She was probably the only woman there who was not a courtesan, servant or close relative of the Wen household, he mused, which intrigued him further. He watched as she shook the folds back from her ample sleeve and, with a small, long-nailed hand, selected a small orange from the bowl before her. Every movement caught his heart like the motions of a ballet, movements that seemed to be etched in life, permanent, with a being of their own.

I am pleased he is here, thought Shen T'ao, avoiding a direct, too obvious glance his way. He is different than when I first met him: taller, golden, as though the aura of a Boddhisattva played about his head. If I feel as I now do at the beginning of the evening, how will I feel when I have drunk wine and poetry, and have disclosed my knowledge, for him only, of the two beasts? How grateful I am that I am not young! For then, I would have had no control, but now, can direct and savor the flow of my own energy. I know that he and I together will break down the gate and fulfill ourselves in the new.

Wen Kuang sought out Wan Su, who was lustily gnawing on a chicken breast, and indicated the two parties clearly oblivious to the rest of the evening's festivities. "Ah ha!" slurped Wan, rubbing his lips against his forearm. "I think our monk friend is hooked! The question is, will he continue to squirm on the barb…."

"Or will he swallow the worm?" Wen completed the thought, with a smirk. "Ah, Wan," he said, enfolding Wan's huge shoulders in layers of sleevecloth, "it is worth a poem just to see them thus, so preoccupied, feigning nonchalance."

"Well, she certainly is feigning nonchalance! But him? He is absorbed in a single thought…."

"The idea of God. The idea of one perfect, inescapable, eternal union…."

"I call it Tao," quoted Wan, guzzling down a bowl of wine.

"I call it…." Wen whispered a vulgarity into Wan's ear and both men exploded in laughter.

The high-pitched voice of a singing girl and the grind of viols died away as Uncle Lu waved his hands from the center of the table. "Please, please! Continue to eat, drink. We have several find poets here this evening, yes?" There was a murmur of approbation throughout the crowd, bowls continuing to clink and chopsticks clicking busily.

As guests rose and mingled, and the atmosphere, loosened by drink, became less rigid, Tu Ming slipped from his place at the table and eased himself to a cushion closer to Shen T'ao. He caught her eye and she smiled warmly. "For you," she mouthed, "I have written a poem." He flushed with pleasure. "I am glad I have come," he mouthed back. "When I am finished," she mimed, "I will leave through the moon gate." She cast her eyes back toward the rear of the hall, where there was a garden for moon watching. He nodded, placed his hand on his heart and bowed low.

As though a spell were broken, Tu Ming felt himself once again full of vitality and eagerly accepted a bowl of wine and honey cakes from a serving boy. With keen interest, he listened to some of the region's brightest poets, including a whimsical doggerel about a bullfrog recited by Wan Su and Uncle Lu's own amateur, but respectable, offering on the rigors of the examination process.

"Tu Ming!" called Uncle Lu suddenly, looking directly his way. Ming started. "My informants (he winked at Wen) tell me that you, too, write poetry. As your payment for attending this fine affair, you must stand now and recite for us from your own oeuvre! " Ming blushed deeply, as the other guests giggled, called out words of encouragement and clicked their chopsticks against their bowls.

Rising, he bowed in several directions, caught Shen T'ao's eye for a split second before she lowered her gaze, and reached into his sleeve.

"Please forgive me for not yet having memorized this new verse, which I composed this morning. It was written to express gratitude for spring after a difficult winter of wandering."

Tu Ming read:

Counting his beads, again and again,

Ten thousand memories, night
And day, the old monk's winter
Spell's smashed by spring's
Bright blast. Abrupt, he jumps
And opens crusty eyes. A silkworm
Wiggles in his tea. He smiles,
And sighs.

Murmurs of appreciation rose from those near-by; several tapped their chopsticks appreciatively against their wine bowls. Wan Su coughed and scuffed the floor with his toe; the poem was not great, but certainly better than he expected from the young monk. Wen Kuang smiled warmly and gave Tu Ming a little bow, which the poet returned.

"May I?" asked Shen T'ao boldly from the other end of the table. Several guests wrinkled their noses in annoyance, while others, familiar with Shen T'ao's reputation, nodded their assent. Shen T'ao leaned jauntily to one side, looked cooly at Tu Ming, her friends and then recited clearly, to no one in particular:

Beads of sweat, like dewdrops, ring
His head. Ten thousand thrusts, by
Day, by night, and no release. His silk
Clad partner knows exactly when
To hook the worm. It's her command.
A sudden gasp and groans of exultation rise:
The unity complete, so sweet, between
Their eyes.

A low roar rumbled through the hall like the beginning of an earth tremor. Some murmured their appreciation of her spontaneous riposte. Others growled disapproval of the frankly sexual symbolism. Others took offense that what they took to be a purely religious poem was countered by one which suggested carnality. Still others found this juxtaposition all the more reason to appreciate and praise the woman poet.

"I think...." said Wen, with large, comedic eyes, scooping up Shen T'ao under his sleeve, "....you'd better take a powder!"

"It was a boring party," said T'ao, being bundled away as guests argued openly and with increasing volume with each other. "Any way, they aren't angry at me. It's their thoughts, their biases which provoke them!" she cried under the muffling folds of silk.

"Sometimes I feel like your brother or maybe your governess!" said Wen in mock complaint, rolling his eyes. "You are always getting yourself in trouble."

"Here, here!" cried T'ao, elbowing him in the ribs so he would steer her to the moon gate in the rear of the hall. "Just leave me here, I'll be fine. Go back in and see that nothing unpleasant happens in your uncle's house. Go on!"

Wen propped her safely on the other side of the doorway, gave her an affectionately scolding look and returned to the fray. Shen T'ao smoothed out her clothes and, sinking to the floor in a cross-legged position, ran her long fingernails over her hair to rearrange the tousled blossoms. As she sat, her hairpin between her teeth, both hands lost in their tonsorial task, the gate creaked open behind her. There was no other sound. She froze and waited. A hand alit gently on her shoulder.

"I did not know," said Tu Ming softly and very slowly, "that you were knowledgeable in the dual cultivation."

Shen T'ao half smiled but did not turn to look at him. "Nor I you," she said at last, removing the pin from her lips and inserting it cleanly between two plaited braids. She turned her head slightly, upward. "Sit down." He sank to the floor beside her, very gracefully.

"That was not the poem you said you wrote for me," he said.

"It was not," she replied. "But it had the same effect. I ensconced the same message in a pattern which would play yin to your yang."

He looked at her hair and lifted his hand up the nape of her neck to gather a heavy fold of braid cupped in his fingers. He moved closer and inhaled the fragrance of the blossoms. "It was really quite remarkable," he said.

She turned her body and looked directly at him, taking both of his hands in hers and tilting her head slightly, inquisitively. "I learned about your calling from some of your associates," she said. "No, I cannot say. Yes, your Master Wu did have something to do with it!"

"I thought I had wandered here by accident," he said.

"There is chance," she said. "It rules everything: our lives, the sea, the stars. But there are few accidents. You are here thanks to a deliberate, calculated design!"

They sat for some moments in silence, regarding each other. Tu Ming thought he could see his own reflection in her dark eyes. But perhaps it was simply the recognition of a kindred spirit. How handsome he is, thought Shen T'ao, but even when he is old, weathered and toothless, I will want to be near him, for there is something in him which is like a missing part of me.

Ming looked over his shoulder and nodded in the direction of the increasing noise. "Perhaps we had better leave."

"Not perhaps: definitely!" said T'ao with an ironic grimace. "Come. My servant Ma Lung will not be surprised if we arrive together."

Ming raised an eyebrow. "Is she used to your arrival with male guests?"

T'ao returned a cool glance. "I am a master of the dual cultivation, as you will shortly learn. I could not attain this level on my own, any more than you could. And yet, it is not so often, and certainly not recently, that I have been so engaged." And never in my own home, she thought. "Above that, I am a poet. And a woman."

Ming blushed. "Forgive me. Take me with you."

So Shen T'ao rose with him, and did.

*   *   *

Tu Ming sat and waited as Shen T'ao went out to talk to Ma Lung. The room was large, but sparsely furnished. There were several cabinets with scrolls, a bowl of water, a dark, warm rug which would soon be taken out for the season. A single white peony rose in a tall green vase, its large, confused face limp, without resistance, on the edge. There was the scent of pine. Ming closed his eyes and inhaled deeply. It was a scent he could live with forever. But his logical brain kicked in. It had been a while since his practice with Lekshe Tsogyal. His own isolated meditations had been productive and enriching, but how would he perform with an expert of Shen T'ao's calibre? She was so very different than his other partners: more mysterious, less obviously impressed with the White Tiger, Green Dragon, even ironic.

He brusquely swept these thoughts of T'ao's individuality from his mind and focused on the process of mingling sun and moon, heaven and earth, in front of the original cavity of spirit. "My body," he thought, "is the Body of Tao," repeating the formula like a mantra.

"Wake up!" Shen T'ao clapped her hands lightly. She knelt beside him where he sat in the full lotus, warming the column channel between the lower burner and the Supreme Ultimate.

She turned and lit a long, thick stalk of incense in the room's one candle. She placed it in a balsam holder beside her writing table. As she passed by, her long fingers glided over the brushes lined there side by side. They knocked musically together like a wind chime.

Tu Ming watched her every movement as though he were accountable for each with his life.

"Who is your favorite poet?" she asked. "I am fond of Chien Shih-Tao of the Sung Dynasty."

"But he is so unspiritual!"

"He finds spirituality in the common place. His love of the simple things of daily life appeals to me."

Ming thought for a moment, and quoted, ...a fly, the sun on his back, rubbing his legs together, relishing the morning brightness."

T'ao smiled. "Sun and shadow about to shift—-already he knows it, suddenly flies off…

"To hum by another window!"

They laughed. "I am amazed! How many monks know about Ch'en's fly!" she said, sinking beside him. "Not as many as those who know of Chuang-tzu's butterfly, I am sure."

Ming thought back to the ironist and philosopher Chuang-tzu, who wondered if he was a man dreaming he was a butterfly, or a butterfly dreaming he was a man.

"But shouldn't we…"

She put a finger over his lips.

"Shouldn't. Wouldn't. Mustn't. None of that! I still do not know your favorite poet!"

Ming took her finger lightly and pressed it into the kiss forming on his mouth. "I have no favorite," he said. "I am utterly open to your doing."

"But not so open that you are ready to surrender your preconceptions, am I not correct?" She sat back and removed the hair pins so painstakingly adjusted two hours before. He watched as her hair fell down in rivers, in cascades, in ribbons. His mind replayed the scene over and over within seconds so it seemed as though she had unleashed the thick, dark cloud a hundred times.

He felt dizzy and steadied his hand on the rug. He was surprised to find it so soft, thick and resilient. His mind repeated the rote he knew he should obey: draw in the genital organ, close the mouth, touch the palate of the mouth with the tongue. Follow the breathing exercises, lift the eyes to the left. Breath out, eyes to the right. Start to feel the warm glow in the lower tan t'ien.

Shen T'ao looked at him with concern, wistfulness and passion. She placed her hand flat against his chest and felt the measured, controlled breaths. Yes, he knows the technique, she thought. But can we get beyond the technique into the Sublime Unknown?

"Wait," she said, taking a blanket from the cabinet. "Let's go outside. I have a garden and bower where I love to write. It is very secluded. Really!" Tu Ming was annoyed. It was not so easy to get into the rhythm. In addition, the thought of being outside with possible prowlers, animals and insects did not appeal to him. "Come!" she insisted, helping him up and steering him out of the room, along a screened in corridor and out into the night.

The house was elevated on a rocky ledge, separated a good distance from other buildings by trees, bushes and a stream which twisted its way around the back. Shen T'ao looked up at the moon, not quite full, and a panoply of twinkling stars. "The evening star!" she said, pointing to the west. She slipped off her shoes, gathered up her skirt and walked carefully across the gurgling water. Tu Ming followed suit. "Be careful," she cautioned, "it falls down precipitously just about…here!" He stumbled slightly and grabbed her shoulder to steady himself. She laughed and led him the rest of the way. They climbed up the mossy slope and threw themselves on several flat rocks where they sat in moonlight filtered through willow branches, like two speckled trout.

"Back here," said Shen T'ao, like a child taking another to her hidden tree house. They stopped under the branches and brushed aside some rushes. Here in a sheltered clearing was a beautiful cove, bordered with irises, with several large flat rocks. Despite its proximity to the stream, it was dry and inviting. Shen T'ao removed a tinder box from her sleeve and lit the stone lantern. "Here, we are safe. Trust me!" Tu Ming sat down and listened. The water was rhythmic and soft. A few melodious birds still sung far away in the darkness. Shen T'ao cupped an iris in her hands and breathed deeply, taking in the wonderful lemon scent. She pinched off a blossom and wove it into her hair, which stirred like an awakening animal in the light breeze.

Tu Ming reached out and grabbed the edge of her dress and pulled her to him. She sat beside him on the rock, and leaned against him watching the sky.

"How far have you gone in the internal alchemy?" he asked her.

"As far as it is possible to proceed," she said. "I have been fortunate in my teachers. And in my ability to move in literary circles where the latest scholarship is available. Tell me, how far have your studies gone?" She looked at him curiously. "Are you still at the stage where you seek a literal transmogrification, or have you ventured beyond the old ways?"

Tu Ming was taken aback. "The old ways, surely you would agree, are the best!" he said. He looked longingly at her full lips and smooth skin in a face full of character, intelligent individuality and purpose. "The sages of old are the source of this practice."

"I know," she said. "It is true, of course. But what happens when, through the centuries, the key to understanding their teaching is corrupted, misrepresented or lost?"

"Can that occur? When so many have faithfully practiced for so long a time?"

"Political opportunism!" she said. "And revolution, war, exile. Our land has been torn apart a thousand times and each time, the politically powerful have tried to use the path of Tao to their own advantage." She touched his arm and rested her hand on the reassuringly solid form. Despite his angelic appearance, he was real. She wondered if she were going too far in her exposition.

He nodded. "This is true. But surely this has been preserved in the monasteries?"

Shen T'ao shook her head. "Not necessarily. Are you familiar with the scholar Liu I-Ming?"

"But of course!" exclaimed Tu Ming. Shen T'ao sighed with relief. "Of course, my masters discouraged my reading him…"

"All of your masters?"

"Not so much Master Wu. No, not at all, but then, the subject never came up with him. Mostly, my scholastic studies proceeded under the watchful eye of Shan Fei Ch'ing." He paused to reflect. She was leading him somewhere, not exactly where he expected to be led!

"Listen!" she said. A bullfrog plopped from a stone into the stream behind them. They laughed. "He will make sure we are not disturbed!"

Shen T'ao slipped her arm around Tu Ming's waist. He pulled her close, and felt both of their breasts rise and fall in a harmonious pattern. Gently, he lifted her narrow chin and placed his lips over her own, lightly gnawing at the edges. Her tongue softly outlined the shape of his mouth. "It is time," she whispered.

Shen T'ao disengaged herself delicately and spread the blanket over the moss. Tu Ming lay down beside her, and removed the silk which clung possessively to her moist skin. She in turn eased off his tunic and let her delicate hands glide down his chest to his waist and dexterously brushed away the fabric like cobwebs. They lay naked facing each other, damp and fragrant in the uneven light of the moon. After some time, Shen T'ao rolled toward and on top of him and lay on his belly, which was hot with internal fire, and felt the powerful surge of energy and power between them. Tu Ming's fingers followed the curve of her spine, up and down and back again, feeling her ch'i flow within him by osmosis. His eyes were closed in ecstasy, but hers were open, with interest as well as desire. Their mouths met again and they devoured each other.

Every position used in the dual cultivation—the cicada, the deer, the dragonfly—they explored and drained of every possibility, without penetration for several hours. Tu Ming focused as hard as he could on the requisite rounds of breaths, the churning of the wheel of ch'i, the cycle up the spine and down until the stem of his brain quivered with heat. Finally, Shen T'ao rose over him again, in the fish-feeding posture, and using only the anterior muscles, pulled him deep within, deeper into the mystery, the source of all being. The warm breeze breathed over them, so they did not perspire excessively as the fire was concentrated and controlled and rose as one through two.

"It is all a metaphor you know," said Shen T'ao, lowering her lips to his ear. "You need not count."

"What are you talking about?" he sighed, as they spoke with no interruption in activity.

She slid flat against his body and they rolled twice, off the blanket, onto the moss, out of the moonlight, where the darkness was spotted with stars.

"Liu I-Ming," she said, stroking his hair, "demonstrated it with clarity. The alchemy is but a symbol, not a literal," she gasped with exquisite pleasure and then continued, "a literal formula for physical…transformation!"

Tu Ming stopped, a cold sweat forming on his brow. He rose up on locked elbows, looking at Shen T'ao, warm, moist and enraptured beneath his body. Her eyes met his eagerly and danced. She smiled. His mouth opened as though to say something. It was then she saw the light come on in his eyes. He got it, she thought, and for the first time, closed her eyes dreamily and lifted her hips toward his falling weight.

"My God!" he exploded into her ear, collapsing hungrily against her. "I understand at last!"

*   *   *

"You see," she said, stifling a yawn, "it was something you had to experience, not something you could be taught."

He wrapped the blanket tightly over both of their bodies. She laughed. "I feel as though I am in a cocoon!"

"You are!" he said, nuzzling her neck, and abandoning himself to a yawn. Their faces reflected the golden light of dawn. The forest behind them rustled, as though bristling under the morning dew; and all the birds in creation sang.

"It all makes sense now," he said. "The internal alchemy, the external alchemy…it's all the same."

"The Tao is the heart of all things," she said. "Our lives are its heartbeats. There is no need to literally light the furnace or direct an actual fire. The heat we experience occurs when our awareness illuminates the ch'i already orbiting within us."

"Liu-I Ming was right," he said. "My teachers have been blind; they do not understand."

She smiled. "One does. The others? It is a new way of looking at a practice which is thousands of years old. If you had invested 30 years in the literal application of the White Tiger Green Dragon, wouldn't you, too, dismiss an upstart who suggested it was all allegory?"

They were silent, watching pale dawn creep up the sky, chasing the moon.

"No spiritual embryo, no child," he said.

"On the contrary!" she scolded, turning to him and playfully pushing his shoulder. "The moment when you understood, that was your red baby! The awareness that occurred at the moment we rode the green dragon into the Crystal Palace, that was our spiritual child. The embryo is the bud of potentiality within each one of us. When it is born, in a blinding flash of pain and blood and transformation, it is a new spiritual body which we put on and grow within."

"Who," he asked, leaning on one arm, "of my teachers understands?"

"Why, it is Master Wu, isn't that clear to you?"

He frowned. "No, in fact, he is the one I thought was most invested in the dual cultivation as a definitive practice. Are you sure?"

Shen T'ao rolled over on her back and gazed at the sky. The stars were streaking toward the west, curling around the North Star. Horsetail clouds sprawled out like waves behind them, carrying the promise of morn.

"Yes," she said, "it is true. He has left the White Crane, you know. Like you. And taken up a simple life with the woman he has known these many years."

"Shang Po?" asked Tu Ming, astonished. He puzzled for a few minutes, then the light of realization brightened his eyes. "Of course! He hinted at this in our last conversation. So all this...my confusion, madness, dejection, despair and now this (he grasped her wrist) sublime understanding (and kissed her fingers one by one)...all was his plan?"

Shen T'ao laughed. "He certainly had a part in it. But only if our own chemistry was compatible." She was silent again, thinking of Wu's letter, thinking of the other women he had contacted and what they must be thinking. A poem began to take form, one she would work on in the coming days. She thought briefly about where they would live, what they would do, but let the idea slip away. She was tired from the ecstasy of realizing that for which she had always longed.

He rolled into the comfort of her thick hair. Would he still continue as a scribe? Should he write to Master Wu? Did he have a responsibility to teach others the true meaning of the path? His thoughts drifted into dreams, into sleep, under the leafy branches which shielded them from day.

Shen Tao was not awake long after him. But in those moments, she looked high into the trees, dappled with sunshine. The brightening sky, the chorus of birds and whispering insects, the dancing shadows around her all moved rhythmically in time with her heart and the flow of ch'i within her body. It was a song which was not simply aural, but visual as well; a scene which could be tasted and heard and smelled as well as seen.

The words of the Sage drifted through her mind:

The Master keeps her mind
always at one with the Tao;
that is what gives her her radiance.
The Tao is ungraspable.
How can her mind be at one with it?
Because she doesn't cling to ideas.
The Tao is dark and unfathomable.
How can it make her radiant?
Because she lets it.
Since before time and space were,
the Tao is.
It is beyond is and is not.
How do I know this is true?
I look inside myself and see. [*]

Totally engaged in the interconnectedness of being, she experienced a deep, satisfying wave of understanding flow over her. Her eyelids fluttered like a falling leaf and brushed down against her cheek. At peace with all things and her beloved, she slipped gently into the easeful arms of sleep.

---

*   Chapter 21 of the Tao Te Ching of Lao Tzu, tr. Stephen Mitchell, Harper & Row, 1988, New York.

About the Author

Simone Marnier is a scholar-practitioner in the field of Eastern and comparative spirituality. Under another name, she is the author of many published articles, essays, book chapter, reviews and poems dealing with East-West spirituality.

BIBLIOGRAPHY

Blofeld, John, *The Secret and the Sublime, Taoist Mysteries and Magic*, New York: E.P. Dutton & Co., Inc., 1973

Chang Po-Tuan, with commentary by Liu I-Ming, *The Inner Teachings of Taoism*, translated by Thomas Cleary, Boston & London: Shambhala, 1986.

Chia, Mantak, and Chia, Maneewan, *Cultivating Female Sexual Energy*, Huntington, New York: Healing Tao Books, 1986.

Chopel, Gedun, *Tibetan Arts of Love*, introduced and translated by Jeffrey Hopkins with Dorje Yudon Yuthok, Ithaca, New York: Snow Lion Publications, 1992.

Chuang-Tzu, The Complete Works of, translated by Burton Watson, New York: Columbia University Press, 1970.

Kabilsingh, Chatsumarn, *Thai Women in Buddhism*, Berkeley, California: Parallax Press, 1991.

Lao Tzu, *Tao Te Ching*, translated by Gia-Fu Feng and Jane English, New York: Vintage Books, 1972.

Lao Tzu, *Tao Te Ching*, translated by Stephen Mitchell, New York: Harper & Row, 1988.

Lu K'uan Yu, *Taoist Yoga: Alchemy & Immortality*, York Beach, Maine: Samuel Weiser, Inc., 1973.

Willis, Janice D., ed., *Feminine Ground: Essays on Women and Tibet*, Ithaca, New York: Snow Lion Publications, 1987.

Watson, Burton, translated by, *The Columbia Book of Chinese Poetry*, New York: Columbia University Press, 1984.